Itinerant
Observations
in America

Itinerant Observations in America

Edward Kimber

Edited by Kevin J. Hayes

DELAWARE

Newark: University of Delaware Press
London: Associated University Presses

Associated University Presses
440 Forsgate Drive
Cranbury, NJ 08512

Associated University Presses
16 Barter Street
London WC1A 2AH, England

Associated University Presses
P.O. Box 338, Port Credit
Mississauga, Ontario
Canada L5G 4L8

The paper used in this publication meets the requirements of the American National Standard for Permanence of Paper for Printed Library Materials Z39.48–1984.

Library of Congress Cataloging-in-Publication Data

Kimber, Edward, 1719–1769.
  Itinerant observations in America / Edward Kimber ; edited by Kevin J. Hayes.
    p.   cm.
  Includes bibliographical references and indexes.
  ISBN 0-87413-631-8 (alk. paper)
  1. United States—Social life and customs—To 1775. 2. United States—Description and travel—Early works to 1800. 3. Kimber, Edward, 1719–1769—Journeys—United States. 4. British—Travel—United States—History—18th century. I. Hayes, Kevin J. II. Title.
E162.K56   1998
973.2—dc21   97-27973
                                                                  CIP

For J. A. Leo Lemay

Contents

Introduction   11
A Note on the Text   25
Itinerant Observations in America   26
Poems Relating to Kimber's American Journey   66

Notes   97
Bibliography   122
First-Line Index to the Poems   128
Index   129

Introduction

Edward Kimber's *Itinerant Observations in America*, first published sporadically during the mid-1740s in the *London Magazine*, remains a vivid record of life in colonial America. Kimber's descriptions of the natural landscape are filled with poetic imagery while his descriptions of the towns, buildings, and fortifications are realistic and original. For many places he visited, especially coastal Georgia, Kimber's narrative provides unique evidence concerning their contemporary appearance. *Itinerant Observations* and the complementary poems Kimber wrote during his American excursion are highly crafted works written by an accomplished litterateur who would make a living with his pen upon his return to London. His writings show how the people, events, and environment of America could supply the matter from which literature could be fashioned.

Little is known of Kimber's early life before he visited North America. He was born in 1719, the son of Isaac Kimber, a Baptist minister whose preaching was unremarkable and who ultimately left the pulpit to pursue a career as an author, editor, and journalist. Of his numerous literary endeavors, Isaac Kimber's *London Magazine* remains his most important. He began editing the monthly periodical in 1732 and continued to edit it until his death in 1755.[1] Since Edward Kimber turned thirteen the year his father began editing the *London Magazine*, there can be little doubt that during his teenage years he helped with the editorial grunt work and read a wide variety of literature.

The allusions to and quotations from a number of poets within *Itinerant Observations* testify to Edward Kimber's wide reading. Perhaps the most influential poem he read during his adolescence was Richard Lewis's "Journey from Patapsco to Annapolis." His father had found the work in the London *Weekly Register* and reprinted it in the *London Magazine* during spring 1733.[2] The poem so profoundly affected Edward Kimber that he later carried a copy of it throughout his American odyssey. Indeed, Kimber's reference to Lewis within *Itinerant Observations* is one of the poet's best contemporary appreciations. Lewis's brilliant depiction of the American landscape fired young Kimber's imagination and may have, at least partially, inspired him to visit America ten years later.

By the end of 1734 Edward Kimber had begun contributing to his father's magazine. Each of the last four issues for that year and another in early 1735 contain poems he wrote.[3] Kimber's early verse is fairly conventional. He employs idealized, unrealistic themes, hackneyed diction, and rhyming couplets. "The Annual Recess," for example, uses pastoral imagery similar to that used by Alexander Pope in his teenage poem, "Windsor Forest." Kimber was no Pope, but he did respect him and his verse clearly shows Pope's influence.

The best of Kimber's early verse appeared in the May 1742 issue of the *London Magazine,* less than six months before he would leave England for America. The poem, "To the Honourable *****," marks a departure from his more youthful verse because it is based on a real event and composed for a specific purpose. Written to an anonymous friend and apparent mentor who was leaving England to take a great voyage, Kimber's long poem pays tribute by describing what he learned from his departing friend and thus indicates his fondness for belles lettres:

> Here *Butler* lashes, there smooth *Waller* flows,
> And warbles *Saccharissa* love-sick woes;
> And *Cowley* soars aloft to *Pindar's* strain,
> And you e'en feel poor *Dryden* sad complain.
> Here *Shakespear* smiles with frolick native air,
> And see, to *Britons* ever justly dear,
> Our great *Spectators* noble dictates there:
> Gay *Mat,* with all his jocund tales bedight;
> And *Swift,* dear *Swift,* array'd in beams of light;
> And all the witty, virtuous, good and sage,
> That strove t'improve, or lash'd a guilty age.[4]

In his twenty-third year, Edward Kimber left England to visit America, but no evidence survives to identify his specific reasons for going. Richard Lewis's "Journey from Patapsco" may have provided romantic inspiration, but Kimber's own poems about his experience hint that he came to America to join the army and to fight the Spanish. Though it is a dangerous thing to equate the speaker of a poem with its author, most of Kimber's adult verse does appear to be highly autobiographical.

While there are some contradictions within the surviving evidence, Kimber's American journey can be pinpointed with reasonable accuracy. *Itinerant Observations* mentions few dates (a deliberate obfuscation), but many of the poems themselves are dated, and a manuscript itinerary of his trip provides additional clues. He left England in September 1742 and reached New York at the beginning of November.[5] Since his stay in New York coincided with a heavy, early snow, his first impressions were not positive:

> These frozen climes, that meet my view,
> Remind me of the sad adieu,
>   I took of ev'ry fair:
> So gloomy, black and dismal seem'd
> The day, on which the light scarce gleam'd
>   To soften my despair.

His chagrin with the blustery weather soon disappeared as he met Kitty Laurence, a young woman he describes as "Genteel, refin'd, and fraught with wit, / And prudence too, to govern it." He had intended to travel overland from New York to the southern colonies, but the snow made the land journey all but impossible, so, around the middle of November, he said good-bye to Kitty Laurence and sailed from New York. He passed through Assateague Inlet to arrive at Sinepuxent, Maryland, eight days later.[6] Generally a brief journey, the New York to Maryland trip took twice as long as it should have. Kimber vividly describes the perilous voyage in *Itinerant Observations*, a description that, as Richard Beale Davis has noticed, anticipates Edgar Allan Poe's *Narrative of Arthur Gordon Pym*.[7]

From the landing place in Maryland Kimber proceeded overland through Snow Hill and down the Accomac peninsula, crossed the Chesapeake, and reached Yorktown, Virginia, in the last week of November.[8] Kimber lingered in Virginia long enough to visit its capital, Williamsburg (he was not impressed). He left Yorktown on 23 December and arrived at Frederica, Georgia, on St. Simons Island, in the first week of January.[9] There he joined General James Oglethorpe's regiment and became a member of the February-March 1742/3 expedition to St. Augustine, Florida, an adventure which he would describe in the anonymously published *A Relation, or Journal, of a Late Expedition to the Gates of St. Augustine, on Florida. . . . In a Letter to the Reverend Mr. Isaac K———r in London* (London: T. Astley, 1744). The trip was neither a success nor a failure. In fact, very little happened. A contemporary of Kimber's who read his *Relation* explained: "this Narrative, which is made up of an uncommon Mixture of the sublime and picturesque, happens to contain, in Substance, only these few facts, viz., That they sail'd on and sail'd off, march'd on and march'd off; that their Indians got four or five Scalps and lost one; and that the Army in their Return were at first surpriz'd, and afterwards diverted by a Polecat, which they kill'd at last."[10] While this critic was disgruntled by the content of Kimber's *Relation* (he especially disliked Kimber's high praise of Oglethorpe), his comments about Kimber's style are not uncomplimentary. Written in the form of a journal, *A Relation* shows that Kimber kept a diary during his travels; it is polished enough, however, to suggest that he had heavily reworked his trip diary before publication. Consider the following description of a stream where he and other members of Oglethorpe's regiment take a rest break:

> This Brook, we are now solacing our selves by, this charming reviving Rill, is seated between two large Pine-barrens, in a Kind of a Bottom, which is quite obscure, from the Thickets that defend it, on the Side of *Augustine;* and on the other Side, a most delicious Grove of Cypress, Laurel, &c. extends its leafy Honours, into the Air, affording a fine, shady Retreat, from the broiling Beams of the Sun. Here our People, throwing aside their Arms and Clothes, gave Way to the pleasing Rest it afforded them; whilst the crystal Stream was incessantly quaff'd, and every diverting Discourse or mirthful Interlude, so common with Soldiers, took Place; which charm'd the General, who was delighted to see the usual, natural Flow of Spirits in his Men, unassisted by ought, but a Vivacity and Chearfulness, inspir'd by native Courage, Vigour, and Health.[11]

The technique here, which can best be described as a prose rhapsody, Kimber would return to again in *Itinerant Observations* as well as in his novels.[12]

After the valorous yet uneventful campaign, Kimber returned to Frederica, where he continued to serve until the following March at which time he traveled northward through Savannah to Charleston, South Carolina, arriving in the second week of April 1744.[13] Ten days later, he left South Carolina.

Itinerant Observations does not describe his return voyage, but the surviving manuscript itinerary and some poems from the *London Magazine* help fill in the details. The first week of June, he made Foul Island, two days sail from the Orkneys. He was in Edinburgh around the middle of June, left there after a few days, and reached London in the first week of July 1744.[14]

Kimber's American experiences formed the basis for his literary productions during the mid-1740s. Besides arranging publication of *A Relation*, Isaac Kimber, always hungry for copy, published many of the poems his son had sent home in the *London Magazine* during 1743 and 1744. Two articles about Oglethorpe that Edward Kimber contributed to the *London Magazine* shortly after returning to London reveal his ongoing respect for his commander.[15] Finally, *Itinerant Observations in America*, the most important of his literary productions, appeared serially from August 1745 through December 1746.

Itinerant Observations: Composition

It is hard to say precisely what state the manuscript that would become *Itinerant Observations* was in when Edward Kimber returned to Great Britain. He had kept a journal throughout the trip and had begun reworking the narrative into a fuller treatment before he left Georgia. He had already separated the part of his journal that described the expedition to St. Augustine during early 1743 from the rest of the trip diary and had shaped it into the distinct narrative that his father would publish as *A Relation*, a work Edward Kimber dated 29 July 1743. In a footnote within *A Relation* that describes Georgia's Jekyl Island, Kimber wrote, "The Description of one of these Islands infers that of all the rest, and in short, of the whole Colony: So that I shall not enlarge here, but defer any Thing on that Head, till I send you an Account at large of *St. Simon's Island*."[16] Since *Itinerant Observations* contains a lengthy description of St. Simons Island, Kimber was either planning or writing *Itinerant Observations* at the time he completed *A Relation*. Like *A Relation*, *Itinerant Observations* was based on his travel diary. Unlike *A Relation*, however, *Itinerant Observations* abandoned the day-by-day format.

A footnote to the St. Simons portion of *Itinerant Observations* states, "This was written in the Beginning of 1743." That same section, however, mentions the explosion of the powder magazine, an event that occurred on 22 March 1743/4, just prior to Kimber's departure from Frederica. He may have begun the St. Simons portion of *Itinerant Observations* in early 1743, but the later reference shows that he had reworked it since then.

Kimber may have been planning to expand his trip diary into an extensive treatment of the North American colonies. The first installment of *Itinerant Observations* is introduced by an anonymous letter to the *London Magazine*, which was either written by Edward Kimber or his father. The introductory letter explained, "A Young Gentleman, who has made the Tour of most Parts of *America*, is preparing for the Press, *Some New and Curious Observations*, made in several Voyages and Travels in that Part of the Globe." Though the comment suggests that he was planning a greater work, it is probably a ruse. In his subsequent novels, Kimber would prove himself to be a master of feigned veracity. The premise that the contributions to the *London Magazine* that make up *Itinerant Observations* formed part of a greater work yet to be published serves to heighten the significance of the individual installments.

At the point where *Itinerant Observations* shifts from its Georgia scenes to an earlier part of Kimber's journey, which describes his arrival in New York and subsequent adventures in Maryland and Virginia, the "anonymous friend" clarifies the narrative's direction in an introductory epistle to the new installment. The letter provides additional details concerning what Kimber might have written or was planning to write. The "anonymous friend" explains that he is interrupting the narrative at the point where the author arrives in South Carolina because the author's "farther Account of *Carolina*, is much interspers'd with the Reasons of the Disputes then existing between that Colony and the infant Settlement of *Georgia*, which, tho' set in an agreeable and just Light, may not be so proper for your Collection, as it may open a Dispute long since subsided." I suspect this assertion about additional unpublished material is yet another fiction. Kimber, like any good Grub Street writer, made sure that what he wrote got printed. His later writing career suggests that he seldom missed an opportunity to publish his writings or even to reuse previously published material. If he had written about Carolina in detail, it seems unlikely he would have neglected to see the writings into print.

Another letter, also purportedly written by the anonymous friend, appeared after the final installment. It continued the ruse that the published segments formed part of a larger whole. It began:

> I have now sent you what Parts would be agreeable of my Friend's Performance for your *Collection*, and thank you for inserting them. His whole Work, of which these may serve as so many Specimens, will soon be sent to Press, and adorn'd with Draughts of the principal Places he has seen. The Reason I have not sent you his Account of *New York* and *Albany*, is, that they are too diffusive for your Design, and interwoven with several Dissertations, that would be too prolix for your Readers; for which Reason I have also left out the Dissertation on the Tobacco Trade, and several important Matters relative to *Virginia* and *Maryland*, which might not be so properly retail'd out in this Manner. The same Reasons I gave you for not touching further on *Carolina* and its City *Charles-Town*, and other Places; and as to his Voyages to and from *Europe*, Remarks on *Scotland* and the North of *England*, and coasting Voyage from thence, *&c.* they did not come within the Title we first set out under, *viz. Itinerant Observations* in *America*.[17]

There is no indication that the larger work was published, completed or, for that matter, intended. If Kimber were genuinely planning a major treatise on the North American colonies, then other writing projects he began after *Itinerant Observations* took precedence.[18]

Kimber's American experiences left a lasting impression on him. His novels, especially his first two, reflect the trip. *The Life and Adventures of Joe Thompson* (1750) contains numerous references to Virginia, colonial trade, Indians, and tobacco.[19] *The History of the Life and Adventures of Mr. Anderson* (1754) is based on an anecdote he recorded in *Itinerant Observations*.[20] Set at Sinepuxent, Maryland, it tells the story of Tom Anderson, a boy who was "trepanned" from England, brought to Maryland, and sold as a servant to a brutal master who happened to have a charming daughter the same age as Tom. Much of what Kimber learned about the inner workings of a Maryland plantation he used in *Mr. Anderson*. Indeed, the novel provides a good gloss for *Itinerant Observations*.

Altogether, Kimber wrote seven novels and translated one from the French. After his first two novels he wrote *The Life and Adventures of James Ramble* (1755); *The Juvenile Adventures of David Ranger* (1756); *The Life and Extraordinary Adventures of Capt. Neville Frowde of Cork* (1758); *The Happy Orphans* (1759), an English translation of C. P. J. de Crebillon's *Heureux orphelins,* which in itself had been based on an earlier English novel, Eliza Haywood's *Fortunate Foundlings; Maria: The Genuine Memoirs of an Admired Lady of Rank and Fortune and Some of Her Friends* (1764); and *The Generous Briton; Or, The Authentic Memoirs of William Goldsmith* (1765). As Frank Gees Black first noticed, Kimber wrote more novels than his more well-known contemporaries Sarah Fielding, Charlotte Lennox, Charles Johnstone, Frances Sheridan, and Frances Brooke, among many others.[21]

After his father's death in 1755 Edward Kimber took over editorship of the *London Magazine,* which he, in turn, continued until his death. He performed much other literary hackwork during this time. A list of literary productions in Kimber's hand from his manuscript notebook reveals the variety and scope of his other work. Upon reading the notebook Edward Kimber's descendant, Sidney A. Kimber reflected, "It is not difficult to visualize these 'Grub Street' writers of the eighteenth century, scholarly men who, by force of circumstances, eked out a mere pittance writing, correcting, and compiling for the booksellers, and who very often died worn out with anxiety and fatigue."[22] Besides his numerous periodical contributions and novels, Edward Kimber made indexes for periodicals, law books, and histories; translated from the French; wrote how-to manuals; proofread the work of others; and compiled several peerages. Richard Johnson, with whom Kimber was collaborating on a new edition of Thomas Wotton's *The Baronetage of England* at the time of his death, wrote, "He gained a scanty subsistence by compiling for booksellers, and died, worn out with such drudgery, in 1769."[23] To be sure, there was much drudgery involved, but Kimber was proud of his work, and his pride shows through in the index he prepared for the *London Magazine.* While most of his writings in the *London Magazine* appeared anonymously, he boldly revealed his authorship of many (though certainly not all) poems and essays within the index.

The Recognition of Edward Kimber

After Sidney A. Kimber printed extracts from Edward Kimber's manuscript notebook during the 1930s, Frank Gees Black specifically identified and attributed the listed novels to Kimber. Many of the other listed titles, however, have not yet been specifically identified or attributed to Kimber. Subsequent advances in bibliography—most notably the creation of the *National Union Catalog* and the ongoing conversion of bibliographic records to online formats—have made it possible for me to assign several additional works to Kimber that the standard bibliographic references do not attribute to him. Kimber wrote *A Letter from a Citizen of London. . . . Occasioned by the Late Earthquakes* (London: for J. Hinton, 1750)[24]; *The Tradesman's Director; Or, The London and Country Shopkeeper's Useful Companion* (London: W. Owen, 1756)[25]; and *The Universal Pocket-Book* (1760), a kind of compendium for coping in London's burgeoning capitalist society.[26] Edward Kimber also listed *The History of Inland Navigations* (London: T. Lowndes, 1766) in his manuscript notebook. The *National Union Catalog* attributes this work to James Brindley, the great projector of canal navigation, and the ideas the work contains are undoubtedly Brindley's, but the book itself was either edited by Kimber or even written by him based on Brindley's notes. Perhaps Kimber's most influential work was *The Ladies Complete Letter-Writer* (London: T. Lownds, 1763), a compilation that achieved considerable popularity in colonial America.[27] Many other titles that Kimber lists as having written cannot be identified specifically. For example, the list includes many ephemeral works that are impossible to identify with precision because no copies apparently survive.

The fact that these works are attributed to Edward Kimber here for the first time indicates how sluggish the recognition of Kimber's accomplishments has proceeded. During his lifetime his novels achieved a modest amount of success—most went through two or three editions, and some were translated into French—but they were published anonymously and did nothing to further his personal reputation. Still, Kimber's authorship of some of these novels was not unknown to mid-eighteenth-century readers. In a contemporary manuscript note made in the Bodleian copy of the thirtieth volume of *The Monthly Review* on a page containing a review of *Maria*, a contemporary reader has starred "The Author" in the text and written in the margin, "Kimber, author of Joe Thomson."[28]

The contemporary reviews of his novels were mixed. Praise was often stated negatively. *The Life. . . . of Captain Neville Frowde,* for example, one reviewer described as "not the worst of the works of this kind that we have seen."[29] Sometimes the reviewers could be cruel. The most scathing remarks occur in the *Critical Review*'s notice of *The Juvenile Adventures of David Ranger*, a work which, the reviewer found, contained "a heap of ridiculous adventures, and some bad poetry by the author; with scraps of plays, ballads, &c. quoted to eke out a trifling and miserable performance; food for idle templars, raw prentices, and green girls, that support the circulating libraries of this learned metropolis."[30] Despite the sometimes negative reviews, the contemporary response to the novels was often positive, though seldom enthusiastic.

The modest popularity of Kimber's anonymous novels continued until near the end of the eighteenth century. *The Life and Adventures of Joe Thompson* was translated into French and German during the 1760s. New editions of *Joe Thompson* appeared in each decade from its initial publication through the 1780s. Kimber's one-time collaborator Richard Johnson abridged the work for children in 1788.[31] Also that year, *Maria* was translated into Russian and published in Moscow.[32] But Kimber's authorship of the novels was never known beyond a small number of contemporary London literati and was forgotten during the early nineteenth century. Robert Watt's monumental *Bibliotheca Britannica* attributes to Kimber only *The Peerage of England, The Peerage of Scotland, The Peerage of Ireland,* and *The Baronetage of England.*[33] Austin Allibone's *Critical Dictionary of English Literature,* published decades after Watt, supplies no new information.[34] The all-too-brief entry in the *Dictionary of National Biography,* first published in 1892, lists only one novel, *The Life and Adventures of Joe Thompson.* Kimber is not mentioned at all in the *Cambridge History of English Literature,* and Halkett and Laing attribute only *The Peerage of Ireland* to him. Not until the 1962 *Addendum* were Kimber's novels and *A Relation* added to Halkett and Laing.[35]

Itinerant Observations was first reprinted in 1878. It appeared as part of the *Collections of the Georgia Historical Society* and was published separately as well.[36] This edition prompted leading Georgia historian Charles C. Jones to remark, "To the *Itinerant Observations in America* the student will turn with pleasure for early impressions of the province, and especially of its southern confines."[37] *Itinerant Observations* was partially reprinted in the *William and Mary Quarterly* in the early twentieth century, but, like the 1878 edition, this, too, appeared anonymously and without editorial annotations. Worse, the *William and Mary Quarterly* reprint misdated the narrative 1736, a mistake that has sometimes misled subsequent scholars.[38] Not until 1918 was *Itinerant Observations* attributed to Kimber by Leonard L. Mackall, then keeper of the excellent Wymberley Jones De Renne Library.[39] *A Relation* was first attributed to Kimber by his descendant, Sidney A. Kimber, in 1934 and reprinted in 1935. While scholars began recognizing the importance of *Itinerant Observations*, Kimber's authorship still did not become widely known. In an article about Yorktown, Virginia, the eminent Virginia antiquarian, E. G. Swem lengthily quoted Kimber's description of Yorktown but did not cite Kimber's authorship of the work.[40] Furthermore, Thomas D. Clark failed to list *Itinerant Observations* in *Travels in the Old South*, though he did list *A Relation*.[41] And even as late as 1977, two other Virginia historians were citing the work without acknowledging Kimber's authorship.[42]

From the mid-twentieth century, *Itinerant Observations* began to receive attention from scholars in a wide variety of disciplines. The editors of the *Dictionary of American English* recognized the linguistic importance of Kimber's work and cited *Itinerant Observations* several times to illustrate the usage of words that originated in America. In the late 1950s E. Merton Coulter saw that *Itinerant Observations* provided unique information describing the Georgia colony's early years. In his history of the Noble Jones family and their stately Wormsloe plantation, Coulter liberally quoted Kimber's descriptions of the Georgia coast and then explained, "Many other travelers were to come this way in the years that followed, to be entertained there and enjoy its hospitalities and to revel in the natural beauty of this region and to describe it. But none to the equal of Kimber."[43] William M. Kelso found Kimber's *Itinerant Observations* useful for his archaeological explorations of Wormsloe. He explained, "Kimber's description of his visit to 'the Settlement of Mr. Jones' provides the only substantial narrative on the appearance of the plantation."[44] Maryland historians, too, recognized Kimber's significance for their colony's history, and the Maryland section of *Itinerant Observations* was reprinted in the *Maryland Historical Magazine* in the 1950s.[45]

During recent decades the gradual interest in Kimber has continued. His American poems were catalogued and attributed to him in J. A. Leo Lemay's *Calendar of American Poetry*. During the mid-1970s the 1878 edition of *Itinerant Observations* was reprinted with Charles C. Jones's *The Dead Towns of Georgia*. *A Relation* was reprinted as part of the Bicentennial

Floridiana Facsimile series. Several novels were reprinted in facsimile as part of Garland's Flowering of the Novel series. *The History of the Life and Adventures of Mr. Anderson*, though a fictional work, was reprinted as part of the Garland Library of Narratives of North American Indian Captivities. A new edition of *Itinerant Observations* was planned but never completed.[46] Since the late 1970s, *Itinerant Observations* has been cited in articles and books discussing a wide variety of scholarly issues: the comparative method and the stage theory in early American literature, colonial slave dwellings, impermanent architecture in the colonial South, slave behavior in early Maryland, colonial Virginia gardens, and the material culture of the Chesapeake region.[47]

Itinerant Observations as Literature

The order of publication of the periodic installments of Edward Kimber's *Itinerant Observations* does not coincide with the chronological order of his journey. *Itinerant Observations* begins with his Frederica experience immediately prior to his departure for England. The narrative then returns to New York where Kimber first arrived, continues to Maryland and Virginia and, ultimately, reaches Frederica, where his narrative began. There are a number of reasons why Kimber may have chosen to begin his narrative with his Georgia experiences. During the mid-1740s, Georgia was more newsworthy than the other colonies. It was a recently formed colony while the others had been in existence for a century or more. Besides, Georgia occupied a strategic location in Britain's war with Spain. Kimber's readers naturally would have been more interested in any colony that figured in the larger British conflict. Kimber may also have begun with Georgia to establish his authority as a narrator. After all, he had spent much more time there than he had in any of the other colonies and could speak about it with more authority. Quite simply, Georgia may have interested him more than the other colonies. The achronological organization was also convenient: it allowed him to tell the story of his American sojourn without retelling the story of the St. Augustine expedition, which he had already detailed in *A Relation*. It is not that Kimber was averse to repeating himself or republishing previously published material. Rather, I think that he simply did not believe that his martial experiences belonged with his traveler's tales. In "A Letter from a Son," Kimber's poetical version of his American adventures, he also avoided detailing the military expedition.

There is yet another reason why Kimber may have begun the story of his travels in the middle, one that is purely literary. The technique of beginning a narrative in medias res was an epic convention that Milton, most notably, had used with such effectiveness in *Paradise Lost*. Perhaps Kimber began *Itinerant Observations* in medias res to give an epic quality to the story of his American sojourn. To be sure, Kimber was not unaware of epic devices. After all, he quoted Milton twice during the early portions of *Itinerant Observations*. Later in the narrative he quoted Richard Glover's epic poem, *Leonidas*. On the other hand, I may give Kimber too much credit. Suggesting he deliberately used the in medias res technique, I assume he originally designed the narrative as an organic whole. The running head of the first installment in the *London Magazine*, however, is "Description of Frederica." The narrative does not take on the title, "Itinerant Observations in America," until the second installment. When he wrote the first segment, Kimber may have had little concept of the whole narrative.

Besides beginning in medias res, *Itinerant Observations* evidences several other consciously literary devices. Most obvious is Kimber's use of periphrasis, usually a two-word phrase made from a noun and an adjective and often introduced with a definite article. In *Itinerant Observations*, as in so much poetry of Kimber's time, fish become "the finny race," sheep "the fleecy Charge," sleep "downy Repose," and trees "the lofty Oak, with all his kindred Tribe."[48] Further, Kimber sprinkles his prose with snatches of verse, sometimes his own but often that of the leading poets of his day. While I prefer to let Kimber's narrative speak for itself, I cannot help but cite one more example of his descriptive technique. Another literary device, hyperbole, some may find inappropriate to a factual account, but few will quibble with Kimber's use of hyperbole as he describes the Chesapeake as "the noblest bay in the Universe."

Itinerant Observations in America is also important because it inaugurates what would become an important genre of American literature during the next century, the outsider's observations.[49] Previous American travel narratives were largely promotional accounts written to encourage colonization. Kimber's purpose is more artistic than rhetorical. While the promotion literature sought to persuade its readers, Kimber seeks to inform and entertain his. Like subsequent European visitors—Chastellux, Chateaubriand, the Duc de la Rochefoucauld, De Tocqueville, Dickens, and Anthony Trollope—Kimber's point of view remains that of an outsider. Though he lacked the insight of De Tocqueville and the caustic wit of Dickens, Kimber nevertheless produced a delightfully original work. A factual account interspersed with rhapsodic descriptions of the natural environment and containing a thrilling sea voyage, *Itinerant Observations in America* makes a memorable addition to the literary history of the American traveler.

A Note on the Text

THE individual installments that make up *Itinerant Observations in America* are presented here in the same order they appeared in the *London Magazine*. I have eliminated the headings of the separate articles, which simply informed readers that the article continued the work from the previous installment. Some of the articles were numbered when they originally appeared, but Kimber dropped the numbering before he finished the series, so I have eliminated the numbers throughout. In the present edition, the different installments are separated with the section sign, §. The only changes I have made within the text have been silent emendations of typographical errors. For reference to the original essays see the *London Magazine* 14 (August 1745): 395–96; (November 1745): 549–52; (December 1745): 602–604; 15 (March 1746): 125–28; (May 1746): 248; (July 1746): 321–30; (November 1746): 572–73; (December 1746): 620–23. *Itinerant Observations* consists of nine sections. The December 1745 issue of the *London Magazine* contained two sections in one. Kimber himself often annotated his text. Here, I have integrated his annotations with my own, indicating his with the parenthetical "Kimber's note." The texts for the poems that follow *Itinerant Observations* are explained in separate headnotes for each poem.

Itinerant Observations in America

To the AUTHOR *of the* LONDON MAGAZINE.

SIR,

A Young Gentleman, who has made the tour of most Parts of *America*, is preparing for the Press, *Some New and Curious Observations*, made in several Voyages and Travels in that Part of the Globe. I have, out of Regard to your Collection, prevail'd upon him to favour the Publick, now and then, thro' your Channel, with his Descriptions of the most remarkable Places he has visited; which can be no Detriment to his Undertaking: I shall give 'em you, just as, and when I receive them, without Order or Connection.

ANONYMOUS.

FREDERICA, on the Island of St. *Simon*, the chief Town in the Southernmost Part of the Colony of *Georgia*, is nearly in Lat. 31° 15′ North. It stands on an Eminence, if consider'd with regard to the Marshes before it, upon a Branch of the famous River *Alatamaha*, which washes the West Side of this agreeable little Island, and, after several Windings, disembogues itself into the Sea at *Jekyl Sound:* It forms a Kind of a Bay before the Town, and is navigable for Vessels of the largest Burden, which may lie along the Wharf in a secure and safe Harbour; and may, upon Occasion, haul up to careen and refit, the Bottom being a soft oozy Clay, intermix'd with small Sand and Shells.[1] The Town is defended by a pretty strong Fort, of Tappy,[2] which has several 18 Pounders mounted on a Ravelin in its Front, and commands the River both upwards and downwards; and is surrounded by a quadrangular Rampart, with 4 Bastions of Earth, well stockaded and turfed, and a palisadoed Ditch, which include also the King's Storehouses, (in which are kept the Arsenal, the Court of Justice, and Chapel) two large and spacious Buildings of Brick and Timber: On the Rampart are mounted a considerable Quantity of Ordnance of several Sizes. The Town is surrounded by a Rampart, with Flankers, of the same Thickness with that round the Fort, in Form of a Pentagon, and a dry Ditch; and since the famous Attempt of the *Spaniards* in *July* 1742,³ at the N.E. and S.E. Angles, are erected two strong cover'd pentagonal Bastions, capable of containing 100 Men each, to scour the Flanks with Small Arms, and defended by a Number of Cannon: At their Tops are Look-outs, which command the View of the Country and the River for many Miles: The Roofs are shingled,⁴ but so contriv'd as to be easily clear'd away, if incommodious in the Defence of the Towers. The whole Circumference of the Town is about a Mile and a Half, including, within the Fortifications, the Camp for General *Oglethorpe's* Regiment, at the North Side of the Town; the Parades on the West, and a small Wood to the South, which is left for Conveniency of Fuel and Pasture, and is an excellent Blind to the Enemy in Case of an Attack; in it is a small Magazine of Powder. The Town has two Gates, call'd the *Landport* and the *Water-port;* next to the latter of which is the Guard-house and underneath it the Prison for Malefactors, which is an handsome Building of brick. At the North End are the Barracks, which is extremely well contriv'd Building, in Form of a Square, of Tappy-Work, in which, at present, are kept the Hospital, and *Spanish* Prisoners of War: Near this was situated the Bomb Magazine, which was blown up on *March* 22, 1744,⁵ with so surprizingly little Damage.⁶ The Town is situated on a large *Indian* Field: To the East it has a very extensive Savannah, (wherein is the Burial Place) thro' which is cut a Road to the other Side of the Island, which is bounded by Woods, save here and there some opening Glades into the neighbouring Savannah's and Marshes, which much elucidate the Pleasure of looking.⁷ Down this Road are several very commodious Plantations, particularly, the very agreeable one of Capt. *Demery,*⁸ and that of Mr. *Hawkins.*⁹ Pre-eminently appears Mr. *Oglethorpe's* Settlement, which, at Distance, looks like a neat Country Village, where the Consequences of all the various Industries of an *European* Farm are seen.¹⁰ The Master of it has shewn, what Application and unabated Diligence may effect in this Country. At the Extremity of the Road is a small Village, call'd the *German* Village, inhabited by several Families of *Saltzburghers,* who plant and fish for their Subsistence.¹¹ On the River Side, one has the Prospect of a large Circuit of Marshes, terminated by the Woods on the Continent, in Form like an Amphitheatre, and interspers'd with the Meanders of

Abundance of Creeks, form'd from the aforesaid River. At a Distance may be seen the white Post at *Bachelor's* Redoubt, also on the *Main,* where is kept a good Look-out of Rangers.[12] To the North are Marshes, and a small Wood; at the Western Extremity of which are the Plantations of the late Capt. *Desbrisay,*[13] and some others of less Note; together with a Look-out, wherein a Corporal's Guard is station'd, and reliev'd weekly, call'd *Pike's,*[14] on the Bank of the River, from whence they can see Vessels a great Way to the Northward. On the South is a Wood, which is, however, so far clear'd, as to discover the Approach of an Enemy at a great Distance; without it, to the Eastward, is the Plantation of Capt. *Dunbar;*[15] and to the Westward, a Corporal's Look-out. The Town is divided into several spacious Streets, along whose Sides are planted Orange-Trees,[16] which, in some Time, will have a very pretty Effect on the View, and will render the Town pleasingly shady. Some Houses are built entirely of Brick, some of Brick and Wood, some few of Tappy Work; but most of the meaner Sort, of Wood only. The Camp is also divided into several Streets, distinguish'd by the Names of the Captains of the several Companies of the Regiment; and the Huts are built generally of Clapboards and Palmetto's,[17] and are each of them capable to contain a Family, or Half a Dozen single Men. Here these brave Fellows live with the most laudable Oeconomy; and tho' most of them, when off Duty, practise some Trade or Employment, they make as fine an Appearance upon the Parade, as any Regiment in the King's Service; and their exact Discipline does a great deal of Honour to their Officers: They have a Market every Day: The Inhabitants of the Town may be divided into Officers, Merchants, Store-Keepers, Artisans, and People in the Provincial Service; and there are often, also, many Sojourners from the neighbouring Settlements, and from *New York, Philadelphia,* and *Carolina,* on Account of Trade. The Civil Government does not seem yet to be quite rightly settled by the Trustees, but is, at present, administer'd by three Magistrates, or Justices, assisted by a Recorder, Constables, and Tything-Men.[18] The Military is regulated as in all Garrison-Towns in the *British* Dominions. In short, the whole Town, and Country adjacent, are quite rurally charming, and the Improvements every where around, are Footsteps of the greatest Skill and Industry imaginable, considering its late Settlement, and the Rubs it has so often met with; and as it seems so necessary for the Barrier of our Colonies, I am in Hopes of, one Time, seeing it taken more Notice of than it is at present.[19]

§

Per varios casus, per tot discrimina rerum.
Virg.[20]

At the South Point of this Island of St. *Simons,* are the Ruins of the Town of St. *Simons,* destroy'd by the *Spaniards* at their Invasion: By the remaining Vestiges, it must have been a very uniform Place; and the Situation is quite charming, tho' it now makes one melancholy to see such a Desolation in so new a Country.[21] The only Building they left standing, was an House which they had consecrated for a Chapel. How different the Proceedings of the more generous *English!* even in these Parts,[22] who never leave behind them such direful Remembrances; but here religious Fury goes Hand in Hand with Conquest, resolv'd to ruin whom they can't convert. The Fort has some Remains still, and seems to have been no extraordinary Affair; tho' no Place was ever better defended, and the Enemies seem, by their Works and Intrenchments, to have thought themselves wofully mistaken.[23] Down the Beach, to the Westward, is a Look-out of Tappywork, which is a very good Mark for standing over the Bar into the Harbour; and on the opposite Point of *Jekyl* Island[24] is a very remarkable Hammock of Trees, much taken notice of by Seamen on the same Account. Somewhat lower, and more Northerly, is the Plantation call'd *Gascoign's,* which underwent the same Fate with St. *Simons.*[25] An Officer's Commande is station'd at South Point, who disposes his Centries so as to discover Vessels some Leagues at Sea, and upon any such Discovery an Alarm-Gun is fir'd, and an Horseman sent up with Notice to the Head-Quarters, which is nine Miles from this Place. If they appear to make for the Harbour; a perpendicular mounted Gun is fir'd, as a Signal, which, by the Ascent of the Smoke, is a Direction to a Ship a long Way in the Offing, and is a most lucky Contrivance. The Road from hence to *Frederica* is cut through the Woods, and through the Marshes rais'd upon a Causeway. To make a good Horseman in *America,* is no easy Matter, without considerable Practice; and Accidents often happen to the best of us, by the Intricacies of the Tracts and Paths. The Horses are the most hardy Beasts imaginable, and tho' they can't all size with *Eu-ropean* Horses, they make it out in Service.[26]

Nature, in all its gay Varieties, seem'd to open her Charms to delight our Senses, in our little inland Voyage from St. *Simons* Island to the chief Town of the North Part of the Colony. My Mind will ever retain the Diversity of Scenes that presented to our admiring Eyes in this Passage; and now I endeavour to commit some faint Sketches of them to Paper, I am lost, me-thinks, in the prodigious Confusion of Objects, that all at once crowd before me, romantically pleasing, and, as it were, make Imagination sick with Wonder. Here let the Atheist, if such there be, view these rudest Footsteps of a Creator, and own himself convinc'd of his Folly and Absurdity, to suppose Chance the Productor. What a judicious Mixture of Light and Shade in the Landskip! how excellent the Colouring! how art-fully dispos'd the Parts! how conducive to the Harmony of the Whole! Rivers and Creeks, that glide with a peaceful, and, as it were, contented Current, into wide Arms[27] and Breaks of the Sea, which seem indignantly to resist their low and servile Community, forgetting, like some of the Race of *Adam,* that they had the same Original, foaming and lashing the Shores with repeated Fury: The Marshes and Savannas extended along their Borders, dispos'd with so seeming a Regularity, as to make the whole Prospect look like one continu'd Canal, the Effect of the most studious Contrivance: Whilst at a distant View you take in a large Tract of hoary Woods, interspers'd with verdant Spots that bear the Semblance of the most re-freshing Meadows; rustick Grottos, rugged Caverns, mossy Caves, and cooling Cells, seem to border their Sides, Here the lofty Oak, with all his kindred Tribe,[28] clad in Robes of antique Moss,[29] seems, by its venerable Appearance, to be the real Mon-arch of the Woods; the Cedar, sweet as the Cedar of *Lebanon;* the towering ever-green Pine, the fragrant Hickary, the mourn-ful Cypress, and here and there the triumphant Laurel, are seen in full Lustre, and preside over an Infinity of lesser Prod-ucts, that seem to venerate, beneath, their more advanc'd and distinguish'd Neighbours. The savory Sassafras Shrub per-fumes the Air, the Prickly-Pear Shrub offers his tempting Fruit to the Hand, but wisely tells you, by the Points that guard it, not to indulge to Excess; the delicious Mulberry, the swelling Peach, the Olive, the Pomegranate, the Walnut, all combine to furnish out the Paradisiacal Banquet. The Vine, alone, luxuri-antly climbs over the highest Oak, and invites with loaded

Clusters, to partake of his refreshing Juice. Across the Glade trips the timorous Deer, the nimble Squirrel skips from Tree to Tree, and at their Roots, scour thro' the Brakes; the wonderful Possum,[30] the squeaking Raccoon,[31] and Millions of the changeable Lizard. Now Harmony breaths forth her choicest Airs, and Musick fills the vocal Groves: The silver-breasted Mock-Bird diversifies her Note, now briskly chirps, like the soaring Lark, now melts in the softer Strain of saddening Philomel;[32] the magnificent Red-Bird joins in the Chorus, which seems now and then interrupted by the Turtle's melancholy Wailing.[33] Adown the Stream the View is still more enchanting, by the sporting of the finny Race; the shining Mullet, the noble Bas, the Warrior Stingre with his redoubted Tail, the Drum, the nimble Cat-Fish, alternately shoot their Heads above the Waves, in which large Banks of Oysters appear like frightful Rocks;—here the dreadful Alligator sports himself in the Canes, and there the heavy Porpoise rolls in sluggish Wantonness,—Now Night succeeds the Day, which seems just to have withdrawn its Beams, to give Place to new Scenes of Wonder; what clear and serene Skies! how bespangled with those glittering Sparks, those Worlds unknown![34] And now, as *Milton* says, the apparent Queen throws her Silver Mantle o'er the Deep,—Silence seems pleas'd;[35]—but hark,—what a confus'd Multitude of Sounds from yonder Marshes! all the Tumult and Cries of a great City are imitated.[36] Another Way the Hissing of Serpents! Here the Rustling of the Deer amongst the Leaves, in yonder Wood, and now and then the prowling Wolf, with the discontented Bear, more disturb the Stillness of the Night, and make the Air tremble with their superior Voices:[37] What glaring Eyes are those in the neighbouring Thicket, that beam Fire upon us?—we present our Pieces,—we fire, and the whole Country echoes back the Groans.—Streaks of Red and Gold paint the Skies, and now Sol just arises from the Ocean, and is confess'd in our Horizon.

This Voyage took us up six Days on Account of the Halts we made, and our waiting for Tides, and the Winds not much favouring us; tho' the Distance is only about 100 Miles. Our Vessel was an open fix-oar'd Boat, in which we stow'd both Baggage and Provisions, and slept and watch'd by Turns, finding, from being frequently inured to it, no more Incommodity in this Method of travelling and resting, than what we felt from the Sand-Flies, Muskettos, and other Vermin, that, like a Swarm of Locusts, infest the hot Months in these Countries.

The Sand-Fly is so minute an Insect as scarce to be perceivable with the naked Eye, only appearing like the sporting Particles of Dust that float in the Sun-Shine. It even intrudes itself into the Mouth as you breathe, and insinuates into all the small Appertures of your Garments, nor can you any Way fend yourself entirely from them. Muskettos are long sharp Flies, whose Venom, I believe, according to their Bulk, is as baleful as that of a Rattle Snake; I have felt them, and heard their cursed Humming too often for it ever to be obliterated from my Memory.[38] Raising a thick Smother of Smoke is the best Means to drive them from an House or Apartment, against which Pressure their Wings are unable to support them; and with us smoaking Tobacco is generally the Subterfuge. There are Abundance of other Torments in these Climates, as Cock-Roaches, Wood-Ticks, &c. &c. And this Colony is either not so enervated as their Neighbours, or else are poor enough to scorn Umbrellas and Musketto-Nets, as *Jamaican* and *Carolinian* Effeminacies.[39]

Our first Stage, we made *New-Inverness*, or the *Darien*, on the Continent, near 20 Miles from *Frederica*, which is a Settlement of Highlanders, living and dressing in their own Country Fashion, very happily and contentedly. There is an independent Company of Foot of them, consisting of 70 Men, who have been of good Service. The Town is regularly laid out, and built of Wood mostly, divided into Streets and Squares; before the Town is the Parade, and a Fort not yet finish'd.[40] It is situated upon a very high Bluff, or Point of Land, from whence, with a few Cannon they can scour the River: Otherways it is surrounded by Pine-barrens, and Woods; and there is a Rout by Land to *Savannah* and Fort *Argyle*,[41] which is statedly reconnoitred by a Troop of Highland Rangers, who do Duty here.[42] The Company and Troop, armed in the Highland Manner, make an extreme good Appearance under Arms. The whole Settlement may be said to be a brave and industrious People; but were more numerous, planted more, and raised more Cattle before the Invasion, with which they drove a good Trade to the Southward; but Things seem daily mending with them. They are forc'd to keep a very good Guard in this Place, it lies so open to the Insults of the *French* and *Spanish Indians*, who once or twice have shewn Straglers some very bloody Tricks. They have here all Sorts of Garden Stuff, and Game in abundance in the Woods and Marshes; as Ducks, Wild Geese and Turkies,[43] Partridges, Curliews, Rabbits, if one may call them so, for the Rabbits of *America* partake much of the Nature of an Hare, and are very numerous; and the Rivers abound with Fish. We staid here two Days, and in a Day and an half, arriv'd at St. *Catherine's*, which is an Island reserv'd to the *Indians* by Treaty.[44] We found about eight or ten Families upon it, who had several Plantations of Corn. It seems to be a most fruitful Soil, and to have larger Tracts of open Land than any I have observed, and to abound in all Kinds of Game, on which the good *Indians* regaled us, and for Greens, boiled us the Tops of China-Briars, which eat almost as well as Asparagus.[45] When we departed, they gave us a young Bear which they had just kill'd, which prov'd fine eating.[46] Passing over more minute Adventures, which, tho' entertaining to us, would be tiresome elsewhere in the Repetition, we arriv'd in somewhat more than two Days at the *Narrows*, where there is a Kind of *Manchecolas* Fort for their Defence, garison'd from *Wormsloe*, where we soon arriv'd. It is the Settlement of Mr. *Jones*,[47] 10 Miles S. E. of *Savannah*, and we could not help observing, as we passed, several very pretty Plantations. *Wormsloe* is one of the most agreeable Spots I ever saw, and the Improvements of that ingenious Man are very extraordinary: He commands a Company of Marines, who are quarter'd in Huts near his House, which is also a tolerable defensible Place with small Arms. From this House there is a Vista of near three Miles, cut thro' the Woods to Mr. *Whitefield's* Orphan House, which has a very fine Effect on the Sight.[48]

§

The Route from *Wormsloe* to Mr. *Whitefield's Orphan-House* is extremely agreeable, mostly thro' Pine Groves, where we saw the recent Appearances of a Storm of Thunder and Lightning, that happened the Day before. Some of the tallest Trees were riven to their very Roots, and their Branches spread far and wide; others had only some Strips taken off, from Top to Bottom, as regularly as a Lath-maker splits his Laths, and at the Roots there seem'd to be an Aperture in the Ground, as if the igneous Matter had penetrated into the very Bowels of the Earth: Every where the Shrubs and Bushes retain'd the Marks of Fire, and the whole Woods offended the Smell with the sulphureous Taint. In all woody Journeys, in these Countries, you perceive Millions of Trees quite strip'd of their Honours, and burnt up by this Means, and the Ruin spread many Miles. 'Tis, indeed, some Surprize to observe these hurricane Tempests, which rise in a Moment, without Warning, and as soon spend their Fury and subside:—the whole Ocean, in a Foam, breaking Mast-high; the adjacent Woods resounding, thro' their remotest Bounds, with the weighty Ruins, that, as *Milton* says,

> *Bow their stiff necks, loaden with stormy blasts,*
> *Or turn up sheer.—*[49]

Thus the fierce Sons of *Aeolus*, rushing abroad with resistless Force, scour the wild Waste, and drive the fiercest Inhabitants of the Plain to their Caves and Dens. The impetuous Rains almost crush you; the Element is kindled into Flames; and the hoarse Thunder growls with deaf'ning Roar.

It gave me much Satisfaction to have an Opportunity to see this *Orphan-House*, as the Design had made such a Noise in *Europe*, and the very Being of such a Place was so much doubted every where, that even no farther from it than *New England*, Affadavits were made to the contrary. It is a square Building, of very large Dimensions, the Foundation of which is of Brick, with Chimneys of the same, the rest of the Superstructure of Wood; the Whole laid out in a neat and elegant Manner. A Kind of Piazza-Work surrounds it, which is a very pleasing Retreat in the Summer. The Hall, and all the Apartments are very commodious, and prettily furnished.[50] The Garden, which is a very extensive one, and well kept up, is one of the best I ever saw in *America*, and you may discover in it Plants and Fruits of almost every Clime and Kind.[51] The Outhouses are convenient, and the Plantation will soon surpass almost any Thing in the Country. The Front is situated towards Mr. *Jones's* Island,[52] (to which, the Way on any Side is impassable, unless by Boat) to whose Plantation the foremention'd Vista is clear'd, which affords to both Settlements a good Airing and Prospect. We were receiv'd by the Superintendant, Mr. *Barber*,[53] a Dissenting Minister, in a genteel and friendly Manner. They were at Dinner when we arriv'd, the whole Family at one Table, and sure never was a more orderly, pretty Sight: If I recollect right, besides Mr. *Barber*, the *Schoolmaster*,[54] and some Women, there were near 40 young Persons of both Sexes, dress'd very neatly and decently. After Dinner they retir'd, the Boys to School, and the Girls to their Spinning and Knitting: I was told, their vacant Hours were employ'd in the Garden and Plantation-Work. Prepossess'd with a bad Opinion of the Institution, I made all the Inquiries I could, and, in short, became a Convert to the Design; which seems very conducive to the Good of an Infant Colony. And whatever Opinion I may have of the Absurdity of some of their religious Notions, Tenets and Practices, yet so far as they conduce to inculcate Sobriety, Industry and Frugality, they deserve Encouragement from all Well-Wishers of their Country: And, indeed, I could not here perceive any Thing of that Spirit of Uncharitableness, and enthusiastick Bigotry, their *Leader* is so fam'd for, and of which I heard shocking Instances all over *America*.[55]

'Tis near eight Miles from this House to *Savanna*, the Road cut thro' the Woods, which has an hundred Curiosities to delight the attentive Traveller, and is diversified with Plantations here and there, tho' now in no very good Order, for a Reason that will be seen by and by.

§

Savanna is situated on a navigable River, which goes by the Name of the Town, and Vessels of considerable Burden may lie close to the Shore, which is between 40 and 50 Feet above the Water's Edge. One main Street runs thro' the whole Town, from the landing Place. It has very near 350 Houses, Huts and Warehouses in it, beside the publick Buildings, which are, the Storehouse of the Trustees, an handsome Court-House,[56] a Goal, a Guard-House, and a publick Wharf, projected out many Feet into the River. The Streets are wide and commodious, and intersect each other mostly at Right Angles: The whole Town is laid out very commodiously, and there are several large Squares.[57] Many of the Houses are very large and handsome, built generally of Wood, but some Foundations are brick'd. They have Plenty of Water, and very good; and the Soil is dry and sandy, which I reckon the most wholsome in this Country, as the Rains entirely dry up, and leave no noxious Steams, as in a moist, low Situation, like that of *Charles Town*, in *South Carolina*, where the People are much afflicted with Agues, &c.

The Houses are built some Distance from each other, to allow more Air and Garden Room, and prevent the Communication, in Case of any Accident by Fire. The Town is divided into Wards and Tithings, which have their several Constables and Tithing-men. The Magistrates are *three Bailiffs* and *a Recorder*, who have Power to judge in capital Crimes, as well as Affairs of *meum* and *tuum*, in that Part of the Colony. They have a publick Garden, in a very thriving Way, which is a Kind of Nursery for the Use of the Inhabitants.[58] The Town stands about ten Miles from the Sea up the River, (which is navigable some hundred Miles up the Country,) and is, certainly, a very good Harbour, and well seated for Trade. The Land, a considerable Space round the Town, is well clear'd, and the Passages lie open; a handsome Road-Way running above a Mile from it; and making the Prospect very lightsome. The Air is pure and serene, and, perhaps, never was a better Situation, or a more healthful Place. Pity it is, that a Spirit of Opposition to the wholesome Rules this Colony was first established upon, Ingratitude to their great and humane *Benefactor;* an Ignorance of their true Interest, and a cursed Spirit of Dissension amongst themselves, has rendered this sweet Place so much less flourishing than it was at the Beginning of the Settlement; but, it is to be hop'd they will learn to hate one another less, be less prone to Faction and Bickering, and Things may, possibly, still be restored to their pristine State.[59] The Inhabitants may be divided into Magistrates, Planters, Merchants and Store-keepers, Artisans and Servants, besides Sojourners from the Northward and Southward. There are many pretty Plantations in the Country about *Savanna,* belonging to the Inhabitants of that Town, particularly, Col. *Stephen's,*[60] Mr. *Causton's,*[61] &c. A *Light-House* is erected on *Tybee Island,* which is a very good Sea-Mark, and the only one South of *Carolina;* tho' for the Use of the Harbour there is little Occasion for it, at present, there being very little Business stirring.[62]

We set out, in a few Days, in one of *Capt. Jones's Scout Boats,* mann'd by a Party of his *Marine Company,* and had a very pleasant Passage to *Fort Frederick* on the *Island of Port Royal* in *South Carolina,* where we arriv'd in a Day and an half, having passed several Sounds, as *Tybee Sound, Port Royal Sound,* &c.

Fort Frederick has the Name of a Fort; but, considering the Importance of the Situation of it, never was a Place worse kept up; in short, 'tis a Heap of Ruins, and capable of no Defence, the Barracks being the strongest Parts of it.[63] The Artillery are few, and badly mounted. The only Thing worth speaking of in it, is the Garrison, which is a small Party of *Oglethorpe's* brave *Regiment,* who, at this Time, were commanded, by a very worthy young Gentleman, *Ensign Archibald Don.*[64] A whole Company of this *Regiment* was once station'd here, and have left some Marks of their Industry behind them. Three Miles from the Fort, or thereabouts, is the Town of *Beaufort*, the Avenues to which are prodigiously agreeable.[65]

§

To the AUTHOR of the LONDON MAGAZINE.

SIR,

When I proposed first to transmit you some Specimens of my Friend's Performance, I told you I should not observe much Order or Connection;[66] but, however, hitherto there has been a Kind of Order observed, from his Description of *Frederica* to his Arrival at *Beaufort* in *Carolina*;[67] which I must now break in upon, as his farther Account of *Carolina*, is much interspers'd with the Reasons of the Disputes then existing between that Colony and the infant Settlement of *Georgia*, which, tho' set in an agreeable and just Light, may not be so proper for your Collection, as it may open a Dispute long since subsided; and when the Character of a certain Gentleman has been set, by the same Author, in a Point of Light that needs no additional Lustre;[68] and at a Time when Malice itself has ceas'd her Calumnies: Therefore, I shall now transport you to another Scene, and leave what I before spoke of to his own Disposal.

Yours, &c.
ANONYMOUS

Some Account of a VOYAGE from New-York to Sene-puxon in Maryland.

Not being able then, on account of the excessive Severity of the Season, and the Depth of the Snow, which was near 4 Feet, to pursue our Route, by Land, thro' the Province of *Pensilvania*, we took Passage on board a Sloop[69] to *Sene-puxon* in *Maryland*, which is generally a Run of 3 or 4 Days, with the Land close aboard, and a fine level Shore. A Traveller should never depend upon any Thing, but his own Sight, or the Experience of a Friend, for the Character of a Vessel and its Commander: 'Tis as absolutely necessary to have a personal Knowledge of those two principal Points of marine Happiness or Misery, as to consult the Temper of your Wife or Friend, or the Situation of your Villa, before you undertake the uncertain Voyage thro' the tempestuous Ocean of Life. Indeed, these are but transient Ills, you'll say, and you may see plainly the End of them: Very true; but as in an unhappy Marriage, so in a Vessel of bad Trim, and under the Government of an obstinate Steersman, you frequently but end your Anxieties in the Arms of Death. Next to the Pleasure you enjoy in having, at Sea, a good, tight, clean Vessel under you, nothing can be more agreeable than a sociable, humane Skipper, who consults the Ease and Satisfaction of his accidental Family before any selfishly sordid Inclination. Misfortune may be lightned by good Company, and the Charms of Friendship will make Amends even for the Horrors of Famine and the most dreadful Tempests. We had no Reason to complain of our Master, indeed; but of an Illness that confined him to his Cabin the whole Voyage, (which was many Days longer than we expected or desired) and which rendered the only able Seaman we found amongst us of no Service. The Vessel was our greatest Grievance we soon found, being prodigously foul, rotten, and leaky; and a Pack of stupid Planters, the Crew, who never had been 10 Leagues from Land since they were born, increased that Misfortune. Unknowing all this, we went on board as gaily as we would have done into a Packet-Boat, and found the Master in Bed which Inconvenience we readily put up with, as the Voyage was so short and safe, and as he informed us, his Mate was a very able Mariner. Our Complement then was, 6 Hands belonging to the Sloop, 3 Passengers, and 7 Negro Slaves; and after taking some necessary Refreshments from Town, we weigh'd and fell down under *Nurten* Island,[70] and might have taken the Advantage of an immediate North-Wester, to have put out to Sea; but here there happened a great Dispute between the Captain and his strange Associates, and in short they refus'd to run beyond *Sandy-Hook* that Night.[71] It seems they had engaged to come this Trip, and to be paid in the Freight of such Goods, as they bought at *New York* for their Plantation Uses, and so were not absolutely under Command; and were resolv'd to lie under the Windward Shore, to consume half an Anchor of *New England* Rum before they left the Sight of *New York*. Rewards and Menaces were of no Service, so we even made a Virtue of Necessity, and wrapping ourselves in our Bedding, slept quietly till next Morning; but found when we arose, that two of our Negroes had lost the Use of their Hands and Feet by the Frost (which was excessively severe) notwithstanding they were warmly clad, and had the free Use of that necessary Liquor (on these Occasions) Rum, in what Quantity they pleas'd. Our Regret at the Disadvantages we had fallen upon, and which our Time and Occasions would not permit us to remedy, could be equalled by nothing but the Displeasure we felt in leaving that delightful Country, that Land of social Joys and heighten'd Pleasures, that flow'd in upon us during our Stay, notwithstanding the rugged Season. Looking behind me, methinks, the Winter Piece is inexpressibly, tho' mournfully agreeable, the River flowing in a long, long Course, till the Sight loses it in an almost imperceptible Point: On one Shore, the goodly City, all surrounded, as it were, with the Waves, reigns supreme Mistress of the brumal Region, and by its aspiring Fumes, seems to declare itself the proper Resort and Comfort of the Season; below it, as far as Eyes can view, the white Beach extends itself, and above its Borders, the now deserted Country Houses rear their unsocial Chimneys.—On the opposite Shore of *Long-Island*, all bleach'd with Snow, appears the sad Reverse of Spring,—the tuneful Warblers but just, weakly, hop over the unfertile Stubble, and raise themselves to complain, in mournful Chirpings, of their forlorn Condition; nor pour out those Floods of Harmony that erst awaken'd, with enliv'ning Melody, the early Swain. The whole Prospect is as of a large Desart, save that here and there the crawling Fences[72] of the Plantations, and the aspiring Vapours of the humble Cottages, shew the Country to be inhabited; and some Remains of the rich Gifts of *Ceres*, unthoughtfully neglected by the Husbandmen, still betray the Footsteps of vernal Industry, and somewhat alleviate my Wintry Chagrin. At Five in the Evening, we were abreast of *Barnegat*, on the Coast of *New Jersey*,[73] and the next Day, at Noon, we open'd *De la War* River, *Cape Henlopen*[74] bearing S. W. about 12 Miles, and had an Expectancy of a prosperous Voyage; when a contrary Wind springing up, we found our Sloop made nothing of plying to Windward, nor answer'd her Helm, and that she was so leaky that the common Spelling at the Pump would not keep her above Water, so that two Hands were constantly employ'd at that Work, immediately, and without the least Distinction of Persons. It seems, that hoping to meet a speedy Passage, they had neglected telling us of their making so much Water; but now were fain to confess their Folly, and implore our Assistance. 'Twas in vain to argue in such a Case, and Self-preservation excited us to use our best Endeavours. All the next Day we lost Way prodigously, and the cold bleak Weather almost perish'd us: Upon comparing our Reckonings, we found ourselves above 50 Leagues from the nearest Land, which we judg'd to be the most Southerly Part of *New Jersey*. This last twenty-four Hours we were drown'd in an Inundation of Rain, which, however, nothing abated the Wind, which blew with redoubled Fury, and the irritated Waves toss'd us aloft and alow in a most frightful Manner, considering the bad Condition of our Habitation, which had not a sound Plank in her, and the Water pour'd in upon us on all Sides. The next Morning open'd, all wild and tempestuous as the last, and our Distractions were increas'd, by three more of our People being taken violently ill of feverish Disorders, occasion'd by the perpetual Watching, the incessant Labour and the Wet and Cold they were constantly subject to; and still more so, by our Hen-Coop with our Fowls, and 2 or 3 Hogs, which were our only remaining Flesh Provisions, being wash'd overboard, and our Lee Gunnel almost all torn away. We were oblig'd to shift our Loading and Ballast on the other Side, and from this Time could keep no Reckoning; but lay to, under our double-reef'd Main Sail, expecting the worst that could befal us. In shifting the Ballast we found one considerable Leak, which I stopp'd as well as I could with an old Salvage well paid with Tallow, and over it nail'd an old Tin Plate, which gave some little Respite to the Pump. We now began to think seriously of the Danger we were involv'd in, and the Death that seem'd inevitable. We had no Carpenter, nor one Person that understood Sea Affairs by Profession, of the whole Crew left, and in short every Thing was fallen into our Hands; we were but two, and the Negroes were all unable to move, the Frost having so affected their Limbs, as to call for present Amputation; two of them being mortified to the Knees and Shoulders: And here, I must observe, that in general, they are the most awkward, ungain Wretches, in cold Weather, that can be met with, and if not stirr'd up, will sit whole Days shivering in a Corner without moving Hand or Foot: They seem to be form'd only for the sultry Climate they were born in, and those they are principally apply'd to the Use of; tho' when inur'd to a cold one long, they bear it tolerably well. We ourselves now began to feel the Effects before mention'd: But what will not Men undergo—how many Hardships that seem quite impossible to human Strength, to preserve that valuable Blessing,

Life! This Day we had a Kind of melancholy *Memento Mori* presented to us, being the Rudder, Main Yard and Part of the Cutwater of a Ship, which floated along Side us, and soon after the Body of a Seaman, in a Jacket and Trowzers, who seem'd newly to have met his Fate, and who about two Ship's Length from us was devour'd by three or four hideous Sharks. I was glad that none but ourselves were then upon Deck, and we forbore to speak at all of such a disagreeable Sight, which every one is not Stoic enough to contemplate without abandoning himself to fruitless Despair. At Night—may never my affrighted Eyes or my amazed and terrified Ears be Witness to the same—what Horrors were we seized with, and how dreadful our Condition!

> All black above—below all foamy white,
> A horrid darkness, mix'd with dreadful light:
> Here long, long hills, roul far and wide away,
> There abrupt vales fright back th' intruding day.[75]

The Deluges of Rain mix'd with the Waves that continually broke over us, the howling Blasts that rent our Ears—the total Darkness, were nothing to our internal Misery. Delirious Ravings on one Side—expiring Groans on another—and the Calls of Help, which we were unable to give, on another, quite distracted us. Bread, Water, and Rum, were all we had left; these were our Provisions for the Sick, these our only Sustenance; and these decreasing so fast as to promise the Addition of the greatest of all Evils to those we already endur'd. Indeed, had our Fowls been preserv'd, we could not have dressed them, we could keep no Fire, and could find no Cooks, and therefore we contented ourselves with Bread dipp'd in Rum for our Patients, and a Draught of Water after it, and Bread and Water for ourselves. We forbore to see after the Negroes, but nail'd down the Hatches, and left them to the Mercy of Providence; we weaken'd apace, and had no Retreat from the Deck, but lash'd ourselves to some Part of the Quarter-Deck, and slept and watch'd by Turns. Thus we weather'd three more dismal Days and Nights, in the two last of which the Wind shifted to the Eastward, tho' without abating of its wonted Fury. However, we made what Way we could, in our present Trim, every Minute expecting to meet with Destruction. We made, as far as we could guess, near 3 Knots an Hour, not daring all these last 24 Hours to direct our Eyes to our distemper'd Messmates in the

Cabin, some of whom we were pretty sure deceas'd in the
Morning. We shap'd our Course as near as possible, to run in
with the next Land, and the next Morning made Shift, one of
us, weak as we were, to get up to the Mast Head. None can
conceive, with what Rapture we descry'd it all abroad; but we
could not tell where we had fall'n in with it, as not having had
an Observation for a long Time. The unexpected Sight almost
depriv'd us of our Senses with very Joy, and instantaneously,
as it were, the Wind dy'd away, and a gentle Breeze succeeded,
that carried us smoothly to our Mark. We open'd a large Inlet,
which we stood in for, and safely came to Anchor, in 12 Fathom
Water, the Bottom a fine Sand mix'd with small Shells.

§

Thus then we found ourselves, to our excessive Satisfaction,
free from those dire Apprehensions that had so long disturb'd
our Minds, and those Fatigues that had jaded our Bodies, in
this little, uncommonly difficult Voyage. As soon as we had
dropp'd Anchor, we saw several Flats[76] full of Men, whom we
perceived to be our Countrymen; but how was our Joy rais'd
into Admiration, when we were inform'd, that the Place we
were in, and had so miraculously lighted on, was *Ascateaque*
Inlet to *Senepuxon!*[77] We ador'd the Goodness of Providence,
and return'd unfeigned Thanks for our Deliverance; and now
we had Time to contemplate the Beauties of the Scene, and to
indulge this new Satisfaction. The Bay we were in, was open
to the Sea on the Eastward, and on every Side else, landlock'd.
We could plainly now discover the Cries of the industrious
Hind, tending his improving Flock; and on every Side, the
Lowing of Kine, the Bleating of the fleecy Charge, and the
Neighing of the generous Steed struck our Ears; and we ex-
changed for this new Musick, the Jargon of bellowing Winds,
the bursting Rains, and the roaring Thunder. The Beach all
glittering with conchous Riches, and white as the driven Snow,
attracted our Eyes on every Side; the green Marshes and Savannahs, even at this Time, appear'd in fresh Verdure; and the
Woods, from the great Quantities of Ever-greens, seemed to
wear a Summer Hue. Up the Country, the Creeks, whose Meanders we could discern, form'd to the Fancy regular Canals,
rushing Torrents, headlong Cascades, and shining Mirrors; but
to moderate our Satisfaction, and to take off from our too great
and presumptuous Exultation, on the Larboard Shore lay the

melancholy Wreck of a large *Bristol* Man, which had stranded in this Place some Years before. 'Tis impossible to describe the Tortures this Sight gave us, which indeed forc'd Tears from our Eyes, by Comparison with what we had been like to suffer ourselves.

We now examin'd our Cabin Associates, and found only the inanimate Remains of three of them. The others had some Signs of Life, and were convey'd on Shore by the Planters who visited us, and were their Neighbours. A thousand Times they lifted their Eyes up with Astonishment at our forlorn Condition. Our Negroes were our next Concern, and here only two were found alive, and such a Stench of Putrefaction in the Hold, as made it necessary to have Recourse to the usual Preservatives from infectious Smells. Ourselves now were to be consider'd, and as soon as the Relations of our Owner came down to the Sloop to take Charge of her, we embark'd in a Flat for *Golden Quarter.* And now, as if our Ability held out only so long as our Necessity subsisted, we soon felt the bitter Effects of our late Troubles: Frost-bitten from Head to Foot, and feverishly distracted from so long a Privation of downy Repose, we now were almost unable to move any Thing but our deploring Eyes; yet,—Misfortune on Misfortune!—our Barge ranaground about a Mile from the Sloop, at low Water, Eleven o'Clock at Night, and we were forced to lie open and exposed till the ensuing Morning, she was loaden so deep; and then, with some Difficulty, we hove her off the Shelve: And this, in an extreme piercing Frost, finished our Disasters, and served almost to rob us entirely of the little Life remaining.

§

Our kind Correspondent, who has favoured us from Time to Time with an ingenious young Gentleman's Remarks in his late American *Tour, has been so good as to send us the following for this Month; which contains so many remarkable Incidents, and such judicious Observations, as we doubt not will be an agreeable Entertainment to our Readers, who are desired to connect it with the last Account in our* Mag. *for* May, *p. 248.*

> *Now we survey the land that owes its name*
> *To* Charles's *bride,———*
> *And soon we change, for all that sailors dread,*
> *The spritely musick, and the sportful dance;*

Where jocund damsels, and their well pleas'd mates,
Pass the delicious moments, void of care,
And only study how to laugh and love,
Contented, happy, under Calvert's *sway.*[78]

Reliev'd from this Distress, we pursu'd our little Voyage, of about 14 Miles, thro' the several Creeks that convey you to *Golden Quarter;* and we were near 24 Hours before we arrived there, occasioned by our frequent Interruptions, or running upon the Marches, or Oyster-Banks, with which these Streams are prodigiously replete. On every Side, you might discern the Settlements of the Planters, with their industrious Clearings, surrounded by the native Woods of the Country; whilst the distant Curlings of the aspiring Smoak, wantoning in the Breeze, direct your Eyes to the happy Places of their Residence, where they, generally bless'd with Innocence and Chearfulness, a compliant Consort, and a numerous Race at their Boards, enjoy a Life much to be envy'd by Courts and Cities. We gather'd a Fruit, on our Route, called a *Parsimon,* of a very delicious Taste, not unlike a *Medlar,* tho' somewhat larger: I take it to be a very cooling Fruit, and the Settlers make use of prodigious Quantities to sweeten a Beer, which they brew of *Cassena* and divers Herbs, which is vastly wholesome.[79] The *Cassena* is a Shrub, that has a small Leaf, somewhat sharpish, and is so admired, when hot Water is poured on it, that I imagine the importing of it to *England* is prohibited for fear of injuring the Tea Trade. At our Arrival at our Host's, we were put to Bed, and for several Days attended with a Tenderness and Humanity that soon restored our Healths, and our Limbs to their proper Function; when, being furnished with Horses, we addressed ourselves to our first Stage, which was about 20 Miles distant from *Golden Quarter,* called *Snow-Hill.*[80] *Golden Quarter* is a kind of straggling Country Village, but the Inhabitants of that Place and *Senepuxon,* tho' poorer than some of their Neighbours of *Maryland,* occasioned by the Poverty of their Soil, are a perfectly hospitable, sociable, and honest Set of People, and abound in every Necessary of Life, and most of the Conveniencies. In short, they seem to repine only on three Accounts, as all this Side of the Colony does: The one is the Scarcity of strong Liquors; another the extravagant Dues to their Clergy, whom they pay a pretty large Quantity of Tobacco yearly to, by Way of Tithe, for every Head in their Families; and the third, is their paying a larger Quit-rent, which I think they do in *Sterling* Money, than any of their Neighbours under the King's Governors.[81] These Things the poorer Sort feel pretty smartly. To be sure, the Clergy ought to be supported in every Country, independently and decently; and certainly they are an Order of Men that are intirely necessary, whilst they behave soberly and uprightly, to the Well-being of Society, and seem no where more so than in these Countries; but as I take it, there is little Justice in a poor Landholder's being obliged to give him as great an Offering as his opulent Neighbour. But here, as in every other Part of the World, the Complaints are very much regulated by the Pastor's Behaviour: You seldom hear any Grumbling when he is a kind, beneficent, humane, and regular Man, that feels for, and endeavours to supply, both the mental Distresses and Wants, as well as the bodily ones, of the Charge intrusted to him; who never, from a Vanity of Temper, a sour Enthusiasm, or a vain Ostentation of Learning, puzzles and distracts his Hearers, by leading them astray from the plain Paths or Meanings of Christianity, into the eternal Labyrinths and intricate Mazes of Speculation and Mystery; nor sets himself up for an infallible Judge of every Dispute, and the authoritative Decider of every Question; nor, to sum up the whole, *daubs and dresses Religion* (as the Poet says) *which is divinely pure, and simple from all Arts, like a common Mistress, the Object of his Fancy.* The Rum they generally have from their Stores, is the *New-England* Sort, which has so confounded a Goût, and has so much of the Molasses Twang, that 'tis really nauseous; and this held up to a very large Price. Sometimes, indeed, an *European* Vessel lands, to the Gentlemen in the Neighbourhood, a Cargo of another Sort; which, however, never diffuses itself much to those beneath them: In other better settled Parts of *Maryland*, indeed, as about *Annapolis*, and elsewhere, you hear of no Complaints of this Sort, as every Thing is in the greatest Plenty imaginable: So that what I am speaking of, relates principally to *Worcester* County and the Parts adjacent, where the Number of Merchants or Store-keepers is but small. You now and then meet with a Cup of good Cyder, in the Season, here, tho' of a thin fretting Kind. The Beer they brew is excellent, which they make in great Quantities, of *Parsimons*, &c. or *Molasses;* for few of them are come to malting their Corn, of any Kind, at which I was much surprized; as even the *Indian* Grain, as I have found experimentally, will produce an wholesome and generous Liquor. The meaner Sort you find little else but Water amongst, when their Cyder is spent. *Mush*[82] and Milk, or Molasses, *Homine*,[83] Wild Fowl, and Fish, are their principal Diet, whilst the Water presented to you, by one of the bare-footed Family, in a copious Calabash,[84] with an innocent Strain of good Breeding and Heartiness, the Cake baking upon the Hearth, and the prodigious Cleanliness of every Thing around you, must needs put you in mind of the Golden Age, the Times of antient Frugality and Purity. All over the Colony, an universal Hospitality reigns; full Tables and open Doors, the kind Salute, the generous Detention, speak somewhat like the old roast-Beef Ages of our Fore-fathers, and would almost persuade one to think their Shades were wasted into these Regions, to enjoy, with greater Extent, the Reward of their Virtues.[85] Prodigious Numbers of Planters are immensely rich, and I think one of them, at this Time, numbers upon his Lands near 1000 Wretches, that tremble with submissive Awe at his Nod, besides white Servants: Their Pastures bless'd with increasing Flocks, whilst their Yards and Closes boast Hundreds of tame Poultry, of every Kind, and their Husbandry is rewarded with Crops equal to all their Ambition or Desires.

The Planters in *Maryland* have been so used by the Merchants, and so great a Property has been made of them in their Tobacco Contracts, that a new Face seems to be overspreading the Country; and, like their more Northern Neighbours, they in great Numbers have turned themselves to the raising of Grain and live Stock, of which they now begin to send great Quantities to the *West-Indies*. And 'tis the Blessing of this Country and *Virginia*, and fits it extremely for the Trade it carries on, that the Planters can deliver their Commodities at their own Back-doors, as the whole Colony is inter-flow'd by the most navigable Rivers in the World. However, this good Property is attended with this ill Consequence, that being so well seated at home, they have no Ambition to fill a Metropolis, and associate together: They require no *Bourses*, or Meetings about Trade; a Letter will bargain for them, and the general Run of the Market determines the Price of the Commodity. For this Reason, the Capitals, and other Towns in these two Colonies, are very slightly peopled, and very badly situated, and remarkable for little else than the Residence of the Governors, and the Meeting of the three Estates, Governor, Council, and Assembly. The principal Meetings of the Country are at their Court-Houses, as they call them; which are their Courts of Justice, and where as much idle Wrangling is on Foot, often, as in any Court in *Westminster-Hall*. The Lawyers have an excellent Time here, and if a Man is a clever Fellow, that Way, 'tis a sure Step to an Estate. 'Tis Necessity that has driven the Practitioners of the Law hither, from *Europe*, and other Parts of *America*, and I remember few that had not made it very well worth their While. Thus *Innocence* and *Truth*, white-rob'd *Innocence* and heavenly *Truth*, can seldom find a Retreat to dwell in. Distracted with their Adversaries barefaced Attempts, 'tis in vain they seek the most distant Skies: Palevisag'd *Guilt*, and wily *Fraud*, still pursue their flow'ry Steps, determin'd to spare no Means to work their Unhappiness. Wherever you travel in *Maryland* (as also in *Virginia* and *Carolina*) your Ears are constantly astonished at the Number of *Colonels*, *Majors*, and *Captains*, that you hear mentioned: In short, the whole Country seems at first to you a Retreat of Heroes; but alas! to behold the Musters of their Militia, would induce a Man to nauseate a Sash, and hold a Sword, for ever, in Derision. Diversity of Weapons and Dresses, Unsizeableness of the Men, and Want of the least Grain of Discipline in their Officers or them, make the whole Scene little better than *Dryden* has expressed it:

> And raw in fields the rude militia swarms;
> Mouths without hands, maintain'd at vast expence,
> In peace a charge, in war a weak defence:
> Stout, once a year, they march a blust'ring band,
> And ever, but in times of need, at hand;
> Of seeming arms, they make a short essay,
> Then hasten to get drunk, the bus'ness of the day.[86]

Indeed, now, I fancy the *Carthagening* Regiment, by returning some of its Veterans, will give a better Face to these Matters.[87]

Holding Land by the Tenure of defending it, seems to be as antient as Time itself; and certainly nothing can endanger a Country more, than an Army of Mercenaries, who perhaps are quite unconcerned in the publick Property, and have nothing to fight for but their Pay. How necessary then is it, that the Militia in these Colonies should be well disciplined! since they have no regular Troops allow'd them, and cannot well maintain a considerable Body long themselves. Even at this Time they are alarm'd with an *Indian* Excursion, and Numbers are marched towards the Back of the Province to defend the Out-Settlements. Their Government is much respected by them, and one may, on the Whole, say, they are an happy People. The

Negroes live as easily as in any other Part of *America*, and at set Times have a pretty deal of Liberty in their Quarters,[88] as they are called. The Argument, of the Reasonableness and Legality, according to Nature, of the Slave-Trade, has been so well handled on the Negative Side of the Question, that there remains little for an Author to say on that Head; and that Captives taken in War, are the Property of the Captor, as to Life and Person, as was the Custom amongst the *Spartans;* who, like the *Americans*, perpetuated a Race of Slaves, by marrying them to one another, I think, has been fully disprov'd: But allowing some Justice in, or, at least, a great deal of Necessity for, making Slaves of this sable Part of the Species; surely, I think, Christianity, Gratitude, or, at least, good Policy, is concern'd in using them well, and in abridging them, instead of giving them Encouragement, of several brutal and scandalous Customs, that are too much practis'd: Such is the giving them a Number of Wives, or, in short, setting them up for Stallions to a whole Neighbourhood; when it has been prov'd, I think, unexceptionably, that Polygamy rather destroys than multiplies the Species; of which we have also living Proofs under the Eastern Tyrants, and amongst the Natives of *America;* so that it can in no Manner answer the End; and were these Masters to calculate, they'd find a regular Procreation would make them greater Gainers. A sad Consequence of this Practice is, that their Childrens Morals are debauch'd by the Frequency of such Sights, as only fit them to become the *Masters of Slaves*. This is one bad Custom amongst many others; but as to their general Usage of them, 'tis monstrous and shocking. To be sure, a *new Negro*,[89] if he must be broke, either from Obstinacy, or, which I am more apt to suppose, from Greatness of Soul, will require more hard Discipline than a young Spaniel: You would really be surpriz'd at their Perseverance; let an hundred Men shew him how to hoe, or drive a Wheelbarrow, he'll still take the one by the Bottom, and the other by the Wheel; and they often die before they can be conquer'd.[90] They are, no Doubt, very great Thieves, but this may flow from their unhappy, indigent Circumstances, and not from a natural Bent; and when they have robb'd, you may lash them Hours before they will confess the Fact; however, were they not to look upon every white Man as their Tormenter; were a slight Fault to be pardon'd now and then; were their Masters, and those adamantine-hearted *Overseers*, to exercise a little more Persuasion, Complacency, Tenderness and Humanity towards them, it might, perhaps, improve their Tempers to a greater Degree of Tractability.[91] Such Masters, and such Overseers, *Maryland* may with Justice boast; and Mr. *Bull*, the late Lieutenant-Governor of *Carolina*,[92] is an Instance, amongst many, of the same, in that Province: But, on the contrary, I remember an Instance of a late Sea Officer, then resident in a neighbouring Colony, that for a mere Peccadillo, order'd his Slave to be ty'd up, and for an whole Hour diverted himself with the Wretch's Groans; struck at the mournful Sound, with a Friend, I hasted to the Noise, where the Brute was beginning a new Scene of Barbarity, and belabour'd the Creature so long with a large Cane, his Overseer being tir'd with the Cowskin,[93] that he remained without Sense and Motion. Happily he recover'd, but alas! remain'd a Spectacle of Horror to his Death; his Master deceas'd soon after, and perhaps, may meet him, *where the Wicked cease from troubling, and the Weary be at rest:*[94] Where, as our immortal *Pope* sings:

No fiends torment, no christians thirst for gold.[95]

Another, upon the same Spot, when a Girl had been lash'd till she confess'd a Robbery, in mere Wantonness continu'd the Persecution, repeating every now and then these christianlike, and sensible Expressions in the Ragings of his Fury, "*G-d d-mn you, when you go to Hell, I wish G-d would d-mn me, that I might follow you with the Cowskin there.*"

Slavery, thou worst and greatest of Evils! sometimes thou appearest to my affrighted Imagination, sweating in the Mines of *Potosi*,[96] and wiping the hard-bound Tears from thy exhausted Eyes; sometimes I view thy sable Livery under the Torture of the Whip, inflicted by the Hands, the remorseless Hands of an *American* Planter: At other Times, I view thee in the Semblance of a Wretch trod upon by ermin'd or turban'd Tyrants, and with poignant, heart-breaking Sighs, dragging after thee a toilsome Length of Chain, or bearing *African* Burdens. Anon I am somewhat comforted, to see thee attempt to smile under the *Grand Monarque;* but, on the other Side of the *Alpes,* thou again resum'st thy Tears, and what, and how great are thy *Iberian* Miseries! In *Britain,* and *Britain* only, thy Name is not heard; thou hast assum'd a new Form, and the heaviest Labours are lightsome under those mild Skies!

Oh *Liberty,* do thou inspire our breasts!
And make our lives, in thy possession happy;
Or our deaths glorious, in thy just defence.

ADDISON

The Convicts that are transported here, sometimes prove very worthy Creatures, and entirely forsake their former Follies; but the Trade has for some Time run in another Channel; and so many Volunteer Servants come over, especially *Irish,* that the other is a Commodity pretty much blown upon. Several of the best Planters, or their Ancestors, have, in the two Colonies, been originally of the Convict-Class, and therefore, are much to be prais'd and esteem'd for forsaking their old Courses:[97] And Heaven itself, we are told, *rejoices more over one Sinner that repenteth, than over ninety and nine that never went astray.* They tell many Stories of some of these People in these Colonies, one of which I commit to Writing, as I had it from the very Person himself, who is the chief in the Story.

Above 60 Years ago, Capt._____, Master of_____, walking thro' *Lincoln's Inn-Fields,* beheld a very pretty Child, about six Years of Age, bewailing himself for the Loss of his Father, whom he had some how or other stray'd from: He sooth'd the Child, persuaded him to dry his Tears, and told him he had Orders from his Father, who was just set out for the Country, to bring him to him. The innocent Victim, without Thought of Harm, follow'd his Deliverer, as he thought him, who carry'd him in the Stage Coach to *Bristol,* and there immediately put him on board his Vessel, which sail'd a Fortnight after for this Part of the World. Still fed up with Hopes of seeing his Father, and that he was going but a small Trip by Water, where he was, and indulg'd by the Captain in all he desir'd, the Time slipt away, till the Brute made appear, by the vilest Actions, his accurs'd Design: The Lad suffer'd much, but his Innocence render'd him incapable to judge of the Propriety of such Actions, and he was acquiescent. When he arriv'd at the End of his Voyage, being very ill, he sold him to a Planter for 14 Years, for 12 Guineas. The Planter, a Man of great Humanity, taking a Fancy to the Child, heard his simple Tale, and perceiv'd the Villany, but not till the Vessel had sail'd. He enquir'd his Name, and just so much he could tell him, and sent over to advertise him in the publick Papers; but before this Design could be compleated, near two Years elaps'd, from his first being kidnapp'd, when, probably, his Father and Mother were both dead, and, perhaps, the Cause of their Death, this Accident. In short, his Master lik'd the Youth more and more, who was sober and diligent, and marry'd him to an only Daughter, leaving him at his Decease his whole Substance. Thirty Years elaps'd, and tho' under great Pain for his Ignorance of his Parents, yet happy in his Family and Affairs, he liv'd with great Content; when a Ship with Convicts coming in, he went to purchase some Servants, and the Idea of his barbarous Captain was so impress'd in his Mind, that he knew him at first Sight, and bought him eagerly; it appearing, afterwards, a notorious Crime had brought him into those Circumstances, and entirely ruin'd him. As soon as he brought him home, he carry'd him into a private Room, and lock'd himself in with him; but what Words could express the Wretch's Confusion and Astonishment, when he understood whose Hands he had fallen into! for he had no Notion before of the Gentleman's being the same, that, when a Lad, he had us'd so vilely. Struck with Remorse, and the Fear of Punishment, he fell on his Knees and begg'd Forgiveness. 'Twas in vain, he was interrogated about his Master's Parents; he knew as little of them as himself; the Master inrag'd, order'd him to be lock'd into an upper Room, resolving to keep him to the hard Service he deserv'd the Remainder of his Life; but the next Morning he was found stabb'd to the Heart, with a Knife that had been uncautiously left in the Room; and so despairingly finish'd a wretched Life. The Gentleman is now near 70, and very hearty and well.[98]

And now let me address me to my Journey, which lay in a very pleasant Road, thro' the Woods, that every now and then presented you with an opening Plantation: We met an *Indian* Man and Woman upon this Road, who came from a Town of *Whigwahms*, near *Snow-hill*, where they inhabit, in great Peace, with their Neighbours. We pass'd several Branches[99] and Savannahs, and the Road all the Way is pretty much upon the Level, and marshy; the Soil of the upper Grounds a loose reddish Sand or Earth. At our Arrival at *Snow-Hill*, I took up Quarters at an *Ordinary*,[100] and found them very good. The Parson of the Parish, who has the only Brick-House in Town, was a good conversible Man, as was also the Presbyterian Minister, a *Scotchman*, of which Nation great Numbers are settled hereabouts. The Church and all the Houses are built of Wood, but some of them have Brick Stacks of Chimneys: Some have their Foundations in the Ground, others are built on Puncheons or Logs, a Foot or two from the Earth, which is more airy, and a Defence against the Vermin. The Women here are very pretty, and the Men, for the generality, obliging enough. The Town is very irregular, and has much the Aspect of a Country Fair, the Generality of the Houses differing very little from Booths.[101] We staid here only one Day, and the next set forward with hired Horses, not being able to buy any in the Town. The Hire was a *Shilling Sterling per* Day for a Guide. They are good serviceable little Creatures,[102] and travel at a great Rate: The next Night we got to the Line that divides *Maryland* from *Virginia*, being about 30 Miles, thro' a Road whose delightful Scenes constantly refresh'd the Senses with new and beauteous Objects.[103] And here I can't help quoting Mr. *Lewis*, when speaking of another Road in this Colony, he says;

> But now the enclos'd plantation I forsake,
> And onwards thro' the woods my journey take;
> The level road the longsome way beguiles,
> A blooming wilderness around me smiles;
> Here hardy *oak*, there fragrant *hick'ry* grows,
> [104]
> Here stately *pines* unite their whisp'ring heads,
> And with a solemn gloom embrown the shades.
> See there a green *savanna* opens wide,
> Thro' which smooth streams in wanton mazes glide;
> Thick branching shrubs o'erhang the silver streams,
> Which scarcely deign t' admit the solar beams.

And, indeed, I can't help, every now and then, taking him out of my Pocket in this Country; for his descriptive Part is just and fine, and such a Warmth of Sentiment, such a delicate Vein of Poetry, such an unaffected Piety runs thro' the Whole, that I esteem it one of the best Pieces extant. This, with my other dearer Treasure,[105] and my *Euclid*,[106] generally relieves me from a too great Sameness of Prospect, or Frequency of the same Objects.

Here, having brought several Bottles of Wine for the Purpose, we drank Success to *Britain*, His Majesty's Health, and that of the Right Honourable Proprietor, whose great and good Qualities have endear'd him much to the People of this Colony.

There certainly can't be a greater Grievance to a Traveller, from one Colony to another, than the different Values their Paper Money bears; for if he is not studious to get rid of the Money of one Place before he arrives at another, he is sure to be a considerable Loser. The *New-England* Money, for Instance, which is excessively bad, and where, to pay a Six-pence or Three-pence, they tear a Shilling Bill to Pieces, is much beneath the *New-York* Money in Value, and will hardly be got off there without some Person is going into the first nam'd Province. *New-York* and *Pensilvania* often differ about the Dignity of their Bills, and they fall and rise in the different Circulations they take. The *Maryland* Money is generally pretty good, but of a low Value, and this, again, is not taken on the Western Shore of *Chesapeak*, where only Gold and Silver is current: *North Carolina* is still lower than *Maryland*, and *South Carolina* worst of all; for their Money there is so low as seven for one *Sterling*, so that it makes a prodigious Sound; and not only so, but even private Traders there coin Money, if I may use the Expression, and give out small printed, or written circulating Notes, from Six pence to a Pound, and upwards; in which they are, no Doubt, considerable Gainers, not only by the Currency of so much ready Money, without much Expence in making it, but also by Loss, wearing out, or other Accidents.[107] In *Georgia*, again, this Money never passes, for all their Bills are of *Sterling* Value, and will pass all over *America* as well as Bank Notes. There are, I find, some considerable Gains, and Stockjobbing in *America*, by the issuing out, and calling in, their new and old Bills, which I shall not think proper to touch upon.[108]

There are very considerable Numbers of *Roman Catholicks* in *Maryland*, particularly about the Borders of *Pensilvania;* but the Bulk of the Colony is of the Episcopal Persuasion, with a grand Mixture of divers other Sects. The Women are very handsome in general, and most notable Housewives; every Thing wears the Marks of Cleanliness and Industry in their Houses; and their Behaviour to their Husbands and Families is very edifying. You can't help observing, however, an Air of Reserve, and somewhat that looks at first, to a Stranger, like Unsociableness, which is barely the Effect of living at a great Distance from frequent Society, and their thorough Attention to the Duties of their Stations. Their Amusements are quite innocent, and within the Circle of a Plantation or two, they exercise all the Virtues that can raise one's Opinion of the too light Sex. I would premise here, that I am not writing any Thing yet of the more refin'd Part of the Colony, but what I say now is confin'd to a Tract of about 200 Miles; for in some other Parts you'll find many *Coquettes* and *Prudes*, as well as in other Places; nor, perhaps, may the Lap Dog or Monkey be forgotten. Hail delightful Sex! would you divest yourselves of but some few Foibles; would you attend somewhat more to the Knowledge of yourselves, and turn your Eye inwards; had not the rolling Chariot, the shining *Ring,* the *Indian* Exoticks, the *Frenchify'd* Affectation, the gay Coxcomb, more Charms than Knowledge, Decency, Prudence, Discretion and Merit, how happy would you be![109] But to roll on in a continued Round of senseless Impertinence, will never, never, raise you to the Character or Situation of these *American* Wives. My God! what a different View has the Representation! the one a Piece where every Figure on the Canvas glows with native Ease, Grace and Proportion, no artful Heightnings, no absurd Conceit, has debas'd the great Designer, Nature: On the contrary, turn your Eyes this Way; what Figures are these? From what distant Clime were they imported? From the Region of *sickly Whim,* and the Designer sure, like *Rabelais,* was resolv'd to paint some Beings that were too odd to exist any where else: What a Load of Ornaments, and a Glare of Colours, that quite hurt the Eye in looking on the Piece![110] nor is there one truly smiling Stroke, one Grace, nor one Beauty in the whole Delineation.

> What's female beauty, but an air divine,
> Thro' which the soul's unfading lustres shine?
> She, like a sun, irradiates all between;
> The body charms, because the mind is seen.
> INCERT. AUCT.[111]

I should busy myself more in the descriptive Part of my Journal whilst in this Colony, did I not reserve myself, till my Arrival in *Virginia;* for there is such a Connection between the Trade and Nature of the Soil, and the Commodities they raise and export, that one general Account will serve for both: Nor do the two Countries appear much of a different Form; for in the Uplands of *Maryland,* they are as mountainous, and abound in Valleys as much as they do in *Virginia.* For this Reason, I wave those Matters till I arrive there, and insist so much on the Manners and Tempers of the Inhabitants and the Genius of this Country.

They have some considerable Seminaries of Learning in the two Colonies; but *Williamsburgh* College in *Virginia* is the Resort of all the Children, whose Parents can afford it; and there they live in an academical Manner; and really, the Masters were Men of great Knowledge and Discretion at this Time;[112]

tho' it can't yet vie with those excellent Universities, for I must call them so, of the *Massachusetts;* for the Youth of these more indulgent Settlements, partake pretty much of the *Petit Maitre* Kind, and are pamper'd much more in Softness and Ease than their Neighbours more Northward. Those that can't afford to send their Children to the better Schools, send them to the Country School-Masters, who are generally Servants, who, after serving their Terms out, set up for themselves, and pick up a Livelihood by that, and writing Letters, and keeping Books for their illiterate Neighbours. Often a clever Servant or Convict, that can write and read tolerably, and is of no handicraft Business, is indented to some Planter, who has a Number of Children, as a School-Master, and then, to be sure, he is a tip-top Man in his Parts, and the Servant is us'd more indulgently than the generality of them.[113]

As I said before, the young Fellows are not much burden'd with Study, nor are their Manners vastly polite: But the old Gentlemen are generally a most agreeable Set of Companions, and possess a pretty deal of improving Knowledge; nay, I know some of the better Sort, whose Share of Learning and Reading, would really surprize you, considering their Educations; but this, to be sure, must be an after Improvement. One Thing they are very faulty in, with regard to their Children, which is, that when young, they suffer them too much to prowl amongst the young Negros, which insensibly causes them to imbibe their Manners and broken Speech.[114] The Girls, under such good Mothers, generally have twice the Sense and Discretion of the Boys; their Dress is neat and clean, and not much bordering upon the ridiculous Humour of their Mother Country, where the Daughters seem dressed up for a Market.

'Tis an odd Sight, that except some of the very elevated Sort, few Persons wear Perukes, so that you would imagine they were all sick, or going to Bed: Common People wear Woollen and Yarn Caps; but the better ones wear white Holland, or Cotton: Thus they travel fifty Miles from Home. It may be cooler, for ought I know; but, methinks, 'tis very ridiculous.

They are all great Horsemen, and have so much Value for the Saddle, that rather than walk to Church five Miles, they'll go eight to catch their Horses, and ride there; so that you would think their Churches look'd like the Out-Skirts of a Country-Horse Fair; but then, as some Excuse, it may be said, that their Churches are often very distant from their Habitations.[115]

An universal Mirth and Glee reigns in *Maryland*, amongst all Ranks of People, and at set Times, nothing but Jollity and Feasting goes forward: Musick and Dancing are the everlasting Delights of the Lads and Lasses, and some very odd Customs they have at these Merry-makings: You would think all Care was then thrown aside, and that every Misfortune was buried in Oblivion. In short, my Spirits have been sometimes raised so much, that I have almost forgotten I was of another Clime, and have wish'd myself for ever amongst them. Adieu! happy People! For the Favours I have reaped at your Hands, Gratitude shall ever fill my Breast: I leave you but to return again;[116] once more to partake of your Halcyon Feasts, and hearty jovial Mirth.

> For now, with glad'ned eyes, we view the bounds
> Of that fam'd colony, from whence the weed,
> The salutiferous plant, that sends the breast
> From noxious vapours of th' inclement morn,
> Provocative to solid, studious tho't,
> Derives its birth and use; the land that erst
> Employ'd the labours of our virgin queen,
> And still is sacred to *Eliza's* fame.[117]

§

In leaving these Lowlands of *Maryland*, and passing into *Virginia*, you find the Scene greatly alter'd; and Hills and Dales, with more frequent Plantations, seem, entirely, to take off the Rudeness of the Country's Aspect. The Roads, also, thro' the two Counties of *Acomoco* and *Northampton*, save here and there, are equal to most in *England;* tho' not near so commodious, as in the Counties on the other Side of the *Bay.* You pass over several considerable Rivers, and Branches, and find many lofty and commodious Bridges; whilst the same Hospitality, Simplicity and Honesty reigns amongst the Inhabitants, as in the Part of *Maryland* I have just traced: Indeed, you find greater, and more considerable Marks of Opulency; and we begin to regale with excellent Wines, good Brandies and Rum, and, here and there, with *English* Porter, which is imported generally in Bottles. Trade, also, seems to flows in a brisker Channel, and the Stores of the Merchants to be better provided; nor are the Gentlemen a little vain, of their being a Part of the King's Government, and look down with an Air of Contempt, upon the neighbouring Patentee Colonies.[118]

The Inhabitants on the *Western Shore,* are supply'd with prodigious Quantities of Beef, Pork, and Grain from this *Eastern
Shore,* as they call them, by Way of Distinction; to whom they
give, also ironically, the Epithet of *Buckskins,* alluding to their
Leather Breeches, and the Jackets of some of the common People; which is, all over *Virginia,* as great a Reproach, as in *England,* to call a Man *Oaf,* or *Clown,* or *Lubberkin.*[119] This *Eastern
Shore* is a Neck of Land, resembling a *Peninsula,* having its
Junction, in about 40° N. with the Main Land, somewhat above
Annapolis, near *Baltimore* and *Elsinburgh,* upon the Frontiers
of *Pensilvania,* where the *Delaware Bay,* and *River,* forms, to
the East, and the Heads of *Chesapeak Bay,* to the Westward,
a Kind of *Isthmus;* and thence, trending away *South-Easterly*
terminates at *Cape Charles,* nearly in Lat. 37°, and is one of the
Abuts, that confines the noblest Bay in the Universe; tho', with
all Winds it is not so convenient to ride in, as having a dangerous Plenty of Sands, Sholes, and Reefs, that have prov'd very
often full of Distress. In this Bay, the whole Navies of *Great
Britain, Holland,* and *France,* might ride at Anchor; it being,
from *Magidi Bay,*[120] to the Entrance of *York River,* more than 20
Miles over; and into which, a Number of the noblest navigable
Rivers disembogue themselves, which you may, as far as the
Eyes can reach, see overspread with waving Forests of *Euro-
pean* Vessels, and a lesser Tribe, who trade from Shore to
Shore, and exchange their own Products for those of their
Neighbours. The common Harbour for the Men of War, in this
Station, is *Sarah's Creek,* on the *Glocester* Side of *York River;*
which a late Commander, the thrice renown'd Sir *Yel,* Peace
be to his Ashes—render'd as shamefully famous, as ever *Turtle
Bay* was render'd by P_____ or E_____s; or *Hobcaw,* by some
others. But to return; we made two Stages, from *Acomoco*
Court House; lying at *Pongoteag* the first Night, and at the
Ferry House at *Magidi Bay* (where a *Chaloupe* attends to transport Passengers and their Horses to *York, Norfolk, Glocester,
James Town,* or other Parts, at a *Pistole* a Horse and Man) the
second Day, being two Days and an half from the *Line,* the
Distance being more than 100 Miles from *Snow Hill* in *Maryland.* There are no considerable Towns on this Shore, only a
few scatter'd Hamlets, particularly, at the Court Houses of the
two Counties, which renders them far less polite, than the Inhabitants on the other Side of the *Bay,* where large Towns
abound, and, which are the Rendezvous of the several *Tobacco
Fleets* that sail from *Europe;* but to make Amends, it may, with

Regard to their Honesty, and Kindness to one another, and to Strangers, be justly call'd, the *Elysian Fields* of *Virginia*. I shall have again, Occasion to mention this Part of the Colony, I find, when I begin to enter into the Nature of the *Tobacco* Trade.

No sooner the Morning dawn'd, than we rous'd from our Beds, and address'd ourselves to our Voyage, in one of those delicious Mornings, in which *Nature* seems to take Pride, in displaying her whole Profusion of Charms; and when a Wretch must be quite inanimate, not to rejoice with the whole Creation, at the infinite Kindness and Benevolence of Providence. All hail! Eternal Sovereign of the Universe! Low, on this *sandy Beach*, surrounded with these venerable Shades, and whilst the Waves are laving at my Feet, let me adore the great, the awful Dispositions of thy creating Wisdom! Alas! how my Importance droops, and how inconsiderable I appear; when, but now, I imagin'd myself one of the Lords of this Globe, and rashly suggested to myself, that all these mighty Stores of Blessings were intended to solace and delight Mankind alone! But if so, why are the most remote Regions so bespangled with thy Goodness; Regions but lately known, and yet, scarce one ten thousandth Part peopled? My Mind opens—; surely, thy wise Intention was to excite the Benevolence of thy more happy Creatures, and *to make thy saving Health known to all Nations*, by spreading the Knowledge of *true Religion and Virtue*, even amongst the sable Inhabitants of these lovely Desarts.

After being victualled for our Voyage, which generally employs three or four Hours, and we had gotten our Baggage and Part of our Attendants on board, we ourselves step'd into a small *Punt*,[121] and put off to the *Shallop;* which, by Reason of the Shallowness of the Water, lay at Anchor near a Mile from Shore, and beyond a very ugly Reef, on which the Waves broke with great Fury; attended by Scores of *Porpoises*, who were wantoning about us. We had very nearly gained the Vessel, when two of these stupid Hogs came souse against one Side of the *Punt*, and overturn'd us, just upon the Back of the *Shoal*.

§

The Pain we are sensible of in our last Moments, must be very trivial, when no foregoing Apprehension of our Dissolution has intruded itself on our Minds, fraught with all the gloomy Terrors, so naturally representant to us, on this awful Occasion. Here, no real Danger, at first, could be imagin'd; for being good Swimmers, a Circumstance of great Account in travelling in this Country, the escaping on Shore again, could be no great Trouble; but in the very first Stroke, bruising my Arm against the Buoy of the Anchor, I was so disabled, as to be driven with the Tide, precipitately, and with so much Violence, into the Current, running directly out to Sea, that I soon lost all Sense of my forlorn Condition. Reflection, as near as I can guess, did not long remain, and two Seconds put me into the State of an Inanimate. Only, continual Roarings, and various unform'd Sounds, intruded upon my Ears for some Time, and then, as it were, I ceas'd to be. *King of Terrors!* thou perpetual and everlasting Dread of the human Race, in how many different Ways thou surprizest unhappy Mortals! No Fences can keep thee out, and thou work'st thy Purposes, often, with the most unforeseen, and most minute Instruments! Lingering, all pale and emaciated, on a Bed of lengthen'd Sickness; all but the deploring Eye, and the conscious Principle, lost to their Functions; how dreadful the Situation! But, prepar'd by a constant Endeavour to do good, and inspir'd with a Regard to the Dictates of Morality and Virtue, conducted by a humane Turn of Mind; how eligible this quick Transition from Life to Death! Here, then, is one principal Qualification of a Traveller, so to conduct his Steps as to be ready at every Stage, to enter that *Eternal Mansion,* or Resting-Place, where Pains shall lose their Sting, and Cares shall vex no more! Hurry'd down the Stream thus, and quite lost to myself, I had soon been lost to my Friends, had not my worthy Associate pursu'd my floating Coarse, and overtaken it, at near half a Mile from the Vessel: When, instantly, seizing me by one Arm, and getting me on his Shoulders, he recover'd a Canoa, which had been dispatch'd from Shore, after us; and, in my first Signs of recover'd Sense, I found myself in Bed, surrounded by a weeping Crew, and my dear Deliverer spent with Fatigue by me, in a little better Situation than myself.

But ah! thou'rt fled,[122] and now exists no more,
In mortal semblance! dearest shade, attend!
Ah! hover o'er me with thy angel wings!
And chase away the grief that hurts my soul;
Grief, endless grief, for thy untimely fate!
Cou'd rocks and sands, or warring waves, conjoin'd,
With howling winds, or all the hideous tribe
Of savages, that prowl the desart waste;

> Could these and more have wing'd thy latest hour,
> We jointly then had render'd up our breath,
> Happy to fall united! Now alone,
> I wander comfortless from place to place,
> And, like the shipwreck'd mariner, aghast,
> On some curs'd barren shelve, I seek in vain,
> With wandering eyes for help in my despair.[123]

The first Emotion I experienced, was that of the most lively and piercing Gratitude to Providence, and the Arm that saved me from the deep Abyss; that Cave of continued Destructions.[124]

In two or three Days we embark'd, being perfectly recover'd, and address'd ourselves once more to the Passage; and here, how can I help sketching out the various Beauties and Adornments of Nature, that elucidated our pleasing Voyage? Suppose us now near ten Miles from either Shore, about the Meridian of one of the most transporting Days, that could have occurred for us, whilst

> ————every storm
> Is hush'd within its cavern, and a breeze,
> Soft-breathing, lightly with its wings, along
> The slacken'd cordage glides; the sailors ear
> Perceives no sound, thro'out the vast expanse,
> None but the murmurs of the sliding prow,
> Which gently parts the smooth and azure main.
>
> GLOVER[125]

The golden Rays of the Sun darting thro' the Gloom of the surrounding Woods, and reflected upon the translucent Face of the watry Plain, gave so lively a Perspective Draught of the circumjacent Country, that we were at a Loss whether to fix our admiring View upon the Reality, or the Representation.[126] These Woods, every where diversify'd with interspersed Plantations, by their reverend Gloom, seemed the Retreat of some antient *Druids;* nor could I forbear a kind of Reverence for so awful a Scene, really much calculated for a Seat of superstitious Rites and Ceremonies; where not a Sigh of the softest *Zephyr,* but in a mournful, melancholy Whisper, is heard thro' the whole Forest, and seems even to form articulate Sounds: Whilst now and then the long pausing Scream of the *Turky,* or the quick, smart Cry of the *Paroquet,* interrupts the responsive Lays of the *Turtle,* and the rest of the musical Choir, and passes in thrilling Chorus from Grove to Grove, from Brake to Brake; whilst imitative *Echo* fondly retains the Sound.[127] Who can, here, help recalling to his Mind, the *Fauns* and *Satyrs* of the Antients; their Fables of *Diana* and her Virgin Train, and their whole beautiful Decoration of the *Sylvan* Scene? When these Fables were first sung, even the now despoiled and desart regions of *Achaia*, and the Territories of *Italy, Gaul* and *Britain* bore just such an Aspect; so buried in the Depth of almost unpassable Woods, and the Inhabitants of some of them little more civiliz'd than the *Indian* Natives of these Regions. And no doubt, but in Proportion to the Increase of our Colonies, the Manners of the antient Possessors may be polish'd, and their brutal Fierceness tam'd; seeing so many potent Nations are exhausted, already, by their intestine Wars, or Broils with the *Europeans*, that they are in the whole *America* not of half so much Importance as they were 100 Years ago. Nay, many Nations live amongst the *English*, there being several Settlements of them in *New-England, Maryland, Georgia*, &c. and in the first nam'd Place, whole Tribes who have embrac'd the Christian Religion, and have Teachers of their own set apart to the Ministry. Like our Preoccupiers, the Antient *Britons*, the *Indians* perform all religious Ceremonies and Mysteries in the deepest Retreat of the Woods; and inur'd from their Infancy to heroic Idleness, and Hunting for Subsistance, they esteem the open *Savannah* or the Corn-Field, no farther than for Profit, whilst their choice Hours of Pleasure are generally sought in the Shade.[128] I remember to have ask'd the famous *Toanahowi*, so caress'd in *England* some Years ago, by the Royal Family, how he liked that Country? He told me, they were good People, but that it was a poor Country, and he could not live in it, because they had no Woods nor Deer, but what were kept in some Gardens; for so he stil'd the Parks of *England*.[129] But to return: The Infinity of Sloops and Barks that appeared every where around, the fine Vista's up *York* and *James* Rivers, and other navigable Streams, the prodigious Flights of Wild Fowl, that darken'd the Air, all in their native Strains hymning the Great Creator; the *Albicores, Dolphins* and *Porpoises* wantoning on every Side, and a long, long View of the Wide Ocean, with a whole Fleet of Vessels in the Offing, tumbling in the Calm, and reeling their lofty, unsteady Heads; the Lowing of the goodly Kine, the Bleating of the Sheep, the Neighing of the useful Steed, and the Cries of the laborious Husbandman, plung'd us into an admiring Extasy: Nor could we forbear to exclaim, *How manifold are thy Works, O Lord! In Wisdom hast thou made them all! The Earth is full of thy Riches: So is this great and wide Sea, wherein are Things creeping innumerable, both small and great Beasts: There go the Ships*, &c.[130] A delicious Moon-light Night succeeded this brilliant Day, and exhibited still new and more delectable Scenes of Wonder, and Millions of unknown Regions, the Work of an eternal, unbounded Creation. Lost in the Contemplation of these Blessings! Struck with such a Field of Magnificence! Exclamation and Rapture is succeeded by the lowest

> Adoration, and the most unfeigned Praises!
> Where'er we stir, where'er we look or move,
> All, all is him, and every where is *Jove*
>
> LUCAN.[131]

At Eight the succeeding Morning, we discover'd the red Clifts of *York* Town, and the opposite Town of *Gloucester;* and sure, nothing could form a more romantick Sight.[132] The Place being somewhat situated like *Dover*, and the Town standing on a Descent, you can only perceive 3 or 4 Houses at first View, and scarce any Thing presents itself but these steep, sandy Banks, dug into an infinite Number of Holes and Caverns, and the Battery of Guns before the Town upon the Pitch of the Bluff.

York-Town, Capital of the County of that Name, is situated on a rising Ground, gently descending every Way into a Valley, and tho' but stragglingly built, yet makes no inconsiderable Figure.[133] You perceive a great Air of Opulence amongst the Inhabitants, who have some of them built themselves Houses, equal in Magnificence to many of our superb ones at *St. James's;* as those of Mr. *Lightfoot, Nelson*, &c.[134] Almost every considerable Man keeps an Equipage, tho' they have no Concern about the different Colours of their Coach Horses, driving frequently black, white, and chesnut, in the same Harness. The Taverns are many here, and much frequented, and an unbounded Licentiousness seems to taint the Morals of the young Gentlemen of this Place. The Court-House is the only considerable publick Building, and is no unhandsome Structure.[135] The amiable Hospitality I have just pass'd an Eulogium upon, on the other Side the *Bay*, seems on this Shore to have found no great Footing: Schemes of Gain, or Parties of Gaming and Pleasure, muddy too much their Souls, and banish from amongst them the glorious Propensity to doing good. The most considerable Houses are of Brick; some handsome ones of Wood, all built in the modern Taste; and the lesser Sort, of Plaister. There are some very pretty Garden Spots in the Town; and the Avenues leading to *Williamsburgh, Norfolk,* &c. are prodigiously agreeable. The Roads are, as I said before, some of the best I ever saw, and infinitely superior to most in *England.*[136] The Country surrounding is thickly overspread with Plantations, and the Planters live, in a Manner, equal to Men of the best Fortune; some of them being possess'd of 500 or 1000*l.* a Year, Sterling.

Gloucester, Hampton, and *Norfolk,* are Towns of near the same Structure, there being little Difference, save that at the last mention'd Place, a Spirit of Trade reigns, far surpassing that of any other Part of *Virginia.* A great Number of Vessels are fitted out from thence, to trade to the Northward and the *West Indies;* and the Inhabitants are, from their great Intercourse with Strangers, abundantly more refin'd.[137] But before I leave *York* entirely, I should just mention the Battery, that is the Defence of the Town, which at this Time was under the Direction of an aukward Engineer, by Trade a Barber, and is as despicably contriv'd for the Safety of the Place, as it, no doubt, would be conducted in a Time of Danger.[138] Indeed, *Virginia* is quite an open Country to the Incursions of an Enemy, having little to resist an Attack by Sea, but the Men of War station'd there, which are generally two or three. In a Land Expedition from the Natives, or *French* and *Spaniards,* indeed, their Numbers, 'tis hop'd, will always protect them, seeing that they could assemble at the shortest Warning, a Militia of 18 or 20,000 Men.[139] They have also some Forts towards the *Apalaches,* which bridle the *Indians,* and secure Trade with them.

Williamsburgh is a most wretched contriv'd Affair for the Capital of a Country, being near three Miles from the Sea, in a bad Situation. There is nothing considerable in it, but the College, the Governor's House, and one or two more, which are no bad Piles;[140] and the prodigious Number of Coaches that croud the deep, sandy Streets of this little City. It's very surprizing to me, that this should be preferr'd to *James-Town, Hampton,* or some other Situations I could mention. Here the Courts of Justice are held, and with a Dignity and Decorum, that would become them even in *Europe.* The present Lieut. Governor *Gooch* is much beloved by every one, and by his mild and agreeable Disposition, diffuses Content every where around.[141] The Posts that are most stickled for here, are the Office of the Secretary, which is said to be worth 900*l. per Annum;* and the being Naval Officers to the several Counties, which are Places of good Profit.————

—We embark'd at *York,* in a Sloop bound for *Frederica* in *Georgia,* immediately weigh'd, and past *Cape Henry* with a brisk and favourable Gale; but when we were abreast of *Cape Hatteras,* the Wind chop'd about, and drove us for 8 Days successively off the Coast, in the most violent Storms that ever I experienc'd; and having reckon'd it as only a Run of 3 or 4 Days, our Provisions were too small in Quantity for the Time we were likely to remain in this Situation. Add to this, a Vessel that could hardly keep above Water, she was so foul and rotten, and no Hands that could be of Service, but the Master, a Negro Fellow, and a Boy: For our Lading consisted of all the Scum of *Virginia,* who had been recruited for the Service of *Georgia,* and who were ready at every Turn to mutiny, whilst they belch'd out the most shocking Oaths, wishing Destruction to the Vessel and every Thing in her; nor would offer the least Hand to help in this Distress: Nay, they were not to be persuaded even to go upon Deck for the Discharge of Nature; but performing all those Offices below, we began to fear a Plague, as well as Drowning. The Master, on the other Side, in a superstitious Fit, was casting Lots who should be the *Jonah* of the Ship, being sure, he said, there was some Murderer on board; and 'twas with Difficulty we kept him to his Duty, upon not complying with his Request. I shall never lose the Idea of this Creature and his Absurdities! Thus then we pass'd so many Nights and Days in miserable Want and Distress, expecting every Minute when the Sloop would part and founder in the drear Abyss.

> ————see forked glare
> The livid lightning thro' the vast expanse,
> And hark hoarse thunder growls with deaf'ning roar.
> See, born aloft, our mast pervades the skies,
> And now we're bury'd in the gulph below,
> Dreadful vicissitudes![142]

On the Ninth Day in the Morning the Wind happily subsided, and on the Eleventh we found ourselves a-breast of *Cape Fear;* and then, to our great Satisfaction, a Wind sprung up, that in four Days more brought us to the End of our Voyage, weaken'd

with Fatigue, and almost dead with Hunger, having liv'd for
some Time on Biscuit and *Indian* Pease in small Quantities.
We cast Anchor in *St. Simon's* Harbour, and immediately de-
barking, set out for *Frederica*.

> Ours is the useful life, tho' want and anguish,
> Famine, and all the various train of Evils,
> That human nature shrinks at, of conspire
> To check our frailty in the glorious race.[143]

Poems Relating to Kimber's American Journey

1
"Song, at New York"

IN his surviving manuscript notebook, Kimber wrote that he left New York for Maryland on 13 November 1742. This poem's long title, however, gives his date of departure as 11 December. The November date is more consistent with other date references among the surviving evidence. This, the earliest of Kimber's American poems to appear in the *London Magazine* (12 [July 1743]: 352; Lemay, *Calendar*, no. 689), concerns his arrival in New York, his initial disappointment with the city, and his subsequent pleasure upon meeting an attractive young woman whom he calls Kitty in the poem and identifies as "*Miss Kath. Laurence*" in a footnote. He would allude to her in a later poem, "A Letter from a Son" (line 111). Not surprisingly, Kitty embodies the conventional attributes of the feminine ideal that could be found in the numerous conduct books of the day and that Kimber himself would later expound upon in *The Ladies Complete Letter Writer*. The poem remains more important as a record of the stranger's first reaction to New York in wintertime. New York's weather and its inhabitants are cold to him. The double entendre, "raking blades" (line 13) captures the harsh noise of snow shovels on the pavement but also hints that the New York men were rakes and gay blades.

SONG, *extempore, by a young Gentleman now in* America, *at his leaving* New York, Dec. 11, 1742, *in order to proceed to* Maryland.

Tune, *In vain dear* Chloe, *&c.*

FROM native *Britain's* verdant plains,
Where ev'ry joy and pleasure reigns,

I greet this *Indian* shore;
But ah! how much unlike the scene,
That in each *British* glade I've seen,   5
    Whose charms I still adore.

These frozen* climes, that meet my view,
Remind me of the sad adieu,
    I took of ev'ry fair:
So gloomy, black and dismal seem'd   10
The day, on which the light scarce gleam'd
    To soften my despair.

The noisy rout of raking blades,
Remote from reason's friendly aids,
    Provoke my rage and spleen;   15
Unlike those dear and learned friends,
I left, yet for no sordid ends,
    To wed with such wild din.

But see! behold the op'ning sight!
What extasy! what sweet delight   20
    Basks o'er my sick'ning mind!
Sure, this will wond'rously repay,
And chace the odd chagrin away,
    To which I so inclin'd.

'Tis *Kitty*,* she, the blooming maid!   25
Whom not one folly can invade,
    Nor can ill nature taint:
Genteel, refin'd, and fraught with wit,
And prudence too, to govern it,
    She, more than pen can paint.   30

New York no more a desart waste,
I think the dangers small, I've past,
    To hail the seemly pile;
Since here perfection keeps its court,
And ev'ry virtue makes resort: 35
    Ah! would but *Kitty* smile!

Fly swift ye irksome lagging hours,
Transport me swift to yonder bowers,
    And quick return me here*:

Else all my days are sable night,   40
Disturb'd by ev'ry hellish sprite,
    And tortur'd by despair.

                E. K.

7   frozen* Winter-time, when he arriv'd there. (*Kimber's note*)
25 *Kitty,* Miss Kath. Laurence. (*Kimber's note*)
39 here* He then thought he should return to *New York*. (*Kimber's note*)

2
"On the Death of Mrs. Alice Kimber"

Since Edward Kimber left England in September 1742 and did not reach New York until November, Alice, the wife of his brother, had died while he was at sea. This elegy, which appeared in the *London Magazine* (13 [1744]: 43–44; Lemay, *Calendar*, no. 716) uses American scenery, particularly coastal Georgia during a storm, as its starting point. While Kimber's poetic output would greatly decrease as he began other, more lucrative writing projects after his return to London, he would continue to write elegies to commemorate close friends and relatives. Perhaps the most touching are the two he wrote about his father. One appeared in the *London Magazine* 24 (February 1755): 88, and the other appeared in his edition of Isaac Kimber's *Sermons* (1756), xviii–xix.

On the DEATH *of Mrs.* ALICE K——R, *who dy'd in*
Childbed, October 24, 1742.
By her BROTHER *in Foreign Parts.*

SEE dusky clouds, the welkin overspread!
See lightning flash its darts, all fork'd and red!
And hark! hoarse thunders growl around my head!
Whence does all nature feel this dread surprise?
Whence, elemental jars and strife arise?   5
Whence, these drear forms, that croud this sandy shore?
Whence, troubled ocean's irritated roar?
Why does this faintness creep thro' ev'ry part,
And whence, this heavy numbness at my heart?
    Alicia's dead, ah tidings fraught with woe!   10
Let sighs burst forth, and tears incessant flow!

Her, gentle matron, fate has soon remov'd,
Whom all admir'd, and all admiring lov'd.
A form divine, a sweet inviting mein,
Charm'd ev'ry eye, when e'er the fair was seen;   15
Her mind was stor'd with ev'ry milder grace,
Smooth as her voice, and smiling as her face.
    Why fled *Lucina* from the *Elysian* plains,
Nor heard thy deaf'ning cries, nor sooth'd thy pains?
Such cruel pains, as tortur'd beauty knows,   20
When dreaded times advance maternal throes,
    Too good for us, fair angel, you but try'd
This wretched, this unworthy world, and dy'd.
    Uncommon anguish rends a brother's breast;
For you, dear saint, my constant thot's possest.   25
Thro' ev'ry clime, my duty bade me go;
There, best of sisters, went they image too;
Fix'd and imprinted ever on my mind,
So tender, so exalt'd so resign'd.
Much had'st thou suffer'd, and in thy morn of life,   30
Thou duteous daughter, and thou truest wife!
    What grief the parents and the husband feel,
My tearful, speaking sorrows will reveal;
Wailing, they hold thee, ever in their view,
And ne'er can bid thy well known shade adieu.   35
    And where was I, thy doating brother, fled,
When all thy friends stood weeping round thy bed?
In worlds, far distant, fortune had decreed,
The wand'ring youth's lamenting heart should bleed.
Tormenting tho't! but I'll be doubly kind,   40
To that fair cherub, thou hast left behind;
Her infant years shall daily lisp thy name,
And, more improv'd, shall heir thy spotless fame.
    But see, what radiant form attracts my sight,
All floating in the purest fields of light?   45
'Tis hers, the virtuous shade, that, soar'd on high,
Adds still increasing lustre to the sky!
Silence our griefs; severe tho' heaven's decree,
We hail the all dispensing deity.

E. KIMBER

---

18 *Lucina* The daughter of Jupiter and Juno, Lucina was the goddess whom women in labour invoked and who presided over the birth of children.

3

"The Vindication"

In the *London Magazine* (13 [February 1744]: 95–97; Lemay, *Calendar*, no. 723), this poem is signed, "E. Kimber, v. G. L. C." G. L. C. stands for a pseudonym Kimber would use in *A Relation* and elsewhere, G. L. Campbell, the consonants of which strongly parallel those in "Kimber." That he signed this poem with his own name suggests the events which it describes are autobiographical. While at Frederica, he apparently received a letter from a female friend in England who wrote to dissuade him from joining Oglethorpe's regiment and serving in the army. By the time he received the letter, however, he had already enlisted. The poem implies that his English friends and family knew of his plans to join the army before he left England. The context of the poem also suggests that Kimber had given "Maria," the person to whom the poem is addressed, some cause for jealousy and had created some bad feelings among female friends in England before he left. The poem contains references to the Georgia scene, some of which are couched in such deliberately poetic language that Kimber must explain their meaning in footnotes.

To Miss Susanna Maria T———, *of* W——— in C———.
The Vindication: *An* Heroic Epistle, *in Answer to one receiv'd from her,* June 2, 1743. *On the Banks of the* Al[tamah]a.

Thy charming lines, all pleasing, reach my hands,
Whilst yet I linger on these barb'rous strands,
Whilst yet the vast *Atlantic* bounds my view,
And fortune calls me from my lord and you:
Where savage, painted heroes throng to arms,   5
There e'en thy *Strephon* glows at war's alarms;
There honour's glorious motions swell his soul,
And martial thunders all around him roll.
    What nature, great almighty power, ordains,
That sure betides, she all despotic reigns.   10
My father wept, humanely great and good,
And strove to check the sallies of my blood;
But vain his tears, paternal sorrows vain,

Resistless inclination to restrain.
Nor thou, my fair, all gen'rous, sweet and kind,   15
Could'st change the dictates that impell'd my mind;
Tho' ev'ry art my lovely damsel knew,
Tho' ever constant, faithful, just and true.
      And still I tempt the sultry, distant shore,
And still new dangers must thy swain explore;   20
Still faithless foes must feel thy *Strephon's* wound,
Who finds new music in the clarion's sound;
Still I defy old ocean's utmost rage,
And the loud storm, terrific, still engage;
Still treach'rous sands, tho' waving with the wind,   25
Confess the traces that I leave behind;
Still hoary forests, untrod woods, shall smoke,*
And howling desarts harms I still provoke;
Still shall the virgin echo learn to tell
Thy much lov'd name, and all my flame reveal.   30
      For, constant still, thy form attends my sight,
Thy wond'rous form, with still encreas'd delight;
Still my *Maria*, inmate of my breast,
You fill my thoughts, and all my dreams suggest:
Oft, on *Cam's* flow'ry banks, I see you stray,   35
Melt in your arms and all dissolve away:
Oft thy lov'd *Hamilton* and thee I chace,
In sportive mood, and strain the long'd embrace.
Ye speechless joys! too, too refin'd to last,
How fast ye fleet, how soon the bliss is past;   40
With what regret I hail the chearful skies,
When, from the soft enjoyment, forc'd to rise;
Curs'd be the day! which tears me from my bride,
Unlocks my arms, oft thrown from side to side;
But, thrown in vain, the airy phantom flies,   45
Deaf to my pray'rs, and heedless of my cries.
Waking, my fancy paints thy heart sincere,
Thy wisdom, virtue, and thy faith severe;
Thinking, or writing, I invoke thy aid
In ev'ry cool recess and conscious shade: 50
Thus would she think, thus would she talk, I say,
Then, frantic grown, I check my longer stay;
Exclaim, that all thy softness I withstood,
And for uncertain, risk'd a certain good:
Strait I resolve, once more, to tempt the main,   55
And speedy visit *Albion's* cliffs again.

How slow your periods! silent now they trill;
A torrent here, and there the purling rill!
How full of sense! what numbers you refine!
What sentiment and force breathes ev'ry line!   60
    But, lovely maid, why in the heav'nly verse,
Will you, your absent *Strephon*'s faults rehearse?
Why, with such sharpness, does your satire sting?
Thus, the high tow'ring eagle on the wing,
Stoops low, to catch at some poor sordid prize,   65
O'er which, superior, he can tyrannize.
True, lov'd *Maria*, cruel maid, 'tis true,
I've acted things would start your nicer view;
But should you lash those faults, to all unknown,
Which, but to you, I never sure could own?   70
    You sing *Eliza* full of grief and woe,
And all those pains the nymph did undergo;
Her loss of life, her infant's wretched doom,
So early fall'n a victim to the tomb.
Ah! poor *Eliza*, dear avenger, say,   75
Can ought e'er chace her from my breast away?
No, faithful image, there she shall reside
Long as my blood pursues its wonted tide;
Her ills I weep, her anguish I deplore,
And wish th' unhappy wretch I could restore;   80
In some lone corner, free from wasteful strife,
She well should weather her remains of life.
But why, sweet censurer, must you accuse
Me as the cause of all her sad abuse?
For, sure, by what you've heard me often tell,   85
Tho', by her own curs'd arts, the woman fell,
With care, unbounded, did not I attend,
And, undeserving, sooth'd her bitter end,
Clasp'd her cold limbs, beheld the dead'ning eye,
And, thro' my lips, receiv'd her latest sigh.   90
    The blithsome rustic *Anna*, you display,
All unsuspecting, innocent, and gay,
And tell me, to my arts, she fell a prey.
You recommend her to my future care,
Nor are your wishes lost in empty air;   95
The honest girl shall find I'm still her friend,
Whom ev'ry good and happiness attend;
Nor shall her offspring lose its parent's store,
Tho'————should exist no more.

Another nymph *Eliza*, too succeeds,   100
She inly suffers, and *Marthina* bleeds;
And *Robertsina* sends to heav'n her prayers,
To shorten, as you say, my growing years.
Why, let them curse and pray, but learn to mend
Their future lives, and find a peaceful end.   105
For, me, my mind and fortunes still remove,
From such, too sordid for a gen'rous love.
    But ah! fond charmer, tempt not, thus, a rage,
Which all thy sex's arts will ne'er assuage.
Hortensia! say, what, what foul monster dare,   110
With her dispraise, to taint thy list'ning ear?
Hortensia, sure, of all the fair on earth,
To ev'ry baneful influence ow'd her birth;
Surrounded, quite, by darkness and deceit,
Her worth still bright'ned in the drear retreat;   115
Damn'd so a crew, the worst of human kind,
Still she displays a noble strength of mind;
Kind to her friends, forgiving to her foes,
Whence could such rumours spring as you disclose?
What wretch, that foams with envy's yellow slime,   120
Could dare t'accuse *Hortensia* of a crime?
Sure, 'twas *Rufinus*, form'd for ev'ry ill,
Or *Mopsa's* baneful tongue, that ne'er stands still.
But yet I live, to see and urge the day,
When all th' abandon'd gang shall drop away;   125
Shall, worn with want and anguish, pining fall,
Unwept, unpity'd, undeplor'd by all.
Then shall *Hortensia's* worth, sublime, be known,
Whose praise, dispraise, and wrongs I make my own;
For sure, a mother's care she still display'd,   130
And grief, or sickness, found her infant aid;
Her tender soothings lull'd the soul to peace,
And, angel-like, she bid all sickness cease.
Ungrateful, then, if I should hear her name,
Mix'd, thus, with others of a trifling same,   135
Mortals, whom will and appetite confound,
True born from clay, and wretches of the ground.
    I see you're touch'd, your sorrows stand confest,
Let my forgiv'ness give thy passions rest;
I quite forget, that e'er thou didst offend,   140
And once more hail my ev'ry wish's end:
But, my *Maria*, fancies fill'd thy head,

By green-ey'd jealousy, and absence bred.
        Fair virtue's laws, thou know'st, have been my aim,
Witness, for thee, my pure aetherial flame.   145
When did I seize thy loose, unguarded hour,
Or o'er thy f****** stretch a wanton power?
When did I say a thing, and strait deny,
Or when my acts, give my resolves the lie?
When was I sporting with my neighbour's wrong?   150
Or join'd yon mean, yon dirty, servile throng?
        How could I clasp thee, fold thee in my arms,
Gaze on that face, and rove all o'er thy charms!
And lo! I come, one rolling year remains,
In which I wear ambition's glorious chains: 155
Then will I fly to catch the wish'd embrace,
Then will we ev'ry irksome tho't erase;
Chace from our minds, that e'er we were confin'd
To sigh our loves, to billows or the wind;
From shores, to shores remote, our souls convey,   160
Or painful count each tedious absent day.
Mix'd, ever mix'd, shall our ideas flow,
Exchang'd and shar'd, each joy and ev'ry woe.
Then *Cam* shall echo to our mutual song,
As smoothly, murmuringly, he glides along: 165
Our *T*——and *Hamilton*, that darling pair,
Each rapt'rous hour, each blissful day shall share;
And where they smile, auspicious heavens approve,
And where they dwell, all satisfactions move.
Me, duty sever'd from his shelt'ring side,   170
Eternal seas and skies, our roads divide:
He, o'er the eastern desarts, devious strays;
And I, thro' western forests,* track my ways:
Omrahs and gloomy *Rajahs* feast his sight,
Me dreadful *Micos*, ev'ry step, delight: 175
Yet, rack'd with heat and thirst, we hail the skies,
Where dews, nor cramp, nor parching suns arise;
Where liberty and freedom are ador'd,
And freeborn *Britons* draw the avenging sword;
Where *W*——'s towers o'er-top the fertile plain,   180
There, where your *Hamilton* and you complain.
        Adieu my all, that heaven reserves to bless
My nights of extacy and days of peace;
Adieu, whom every softer grace refin'd,

To shine, the admiration of mankind: 185
Adieu *Maria*, for the auspicious gale,
With gladsome blast, has fill'd the swelling sail:
More would I write, and write, and write again,
But winds and tides, nor cries nor tears restrain:
Bear her my tears, ye seas that eastward flow,   190
Waft her my sighs, ye wanton gales that blow.
See, on the beach, thy wretched *Strephon* lies,
Straining still, far away, his streaming eyes;
Much lov'd *Maria!* ev'ry breeze shall say,
Till quite o'ercome, oppress'd, I faint away.   195

E. KIMBER. v. *G. L. C.*

27   smoke,* Alluding to the Custom of our sleeping by Fires, in the Woods, to keep off Wild Beasts. (*Kimber's note*)
173   forests,* Alluding to our Method, in these wild Countries, of finding our Ways by Tracks. (*Kimber's note*)
174   *Omrahs* "A lord or grandee of a Mohamedan court, esp. that of the great Mogul" (*OED*).
174   *Rajahs* "Originally the title given in India to a king or prince; in later times extended to petty chiefs or dignitaries" (*OED*).
175   *Micos* Chiefs of the neighboring Georgia Indians.

4
"Fidenia"

Like "The Vindication," "Fidenia" (*London Magazine* 13 [March 1744]: 147–48; Lemay, *Calendar,* no. 730) is spoken by a lover who fashions himself as "Strephon" and speaks to "Maria." Whereas "The Vindication" attempted to assuage Maria's possibly unfounded jealousies, this poem seems to deliberately provoke her jealousy. Kimber expresses his admiration for "Fidenia," a young African woman he met in Maryland. The poem and its footnotes refer to real people and events which Kimber further explains in *Itinerant Observations.*

FIDENIA*: *Or, the* EXPLANATION
Tune, Love's Goddess in a Myrtle Grove, &c.

1.

YE fair, whose worth I so esteem,
　　Who sport on *Britain's* vivid plains,

Still may your smiles upon me gleam,
    For still your lover wears your chains.
Think not, tho' longer I endure   5
    This tedious absence from your eyes,
That time, or distance, e'er can cure
    Those passions that from you take rise.

2.

Tho' sweet *Fidenia*, born of kings,
    From *Afric*'s shores, attracts my sight;   10
What tho' her praise, your *Strephon* sings,
    And eager grasps the new delight?
What tho' her soft and jetty hue
    Gives yet unfelt, untasted joy?
Remembrance speaks such charms in you,   15
    As all her blandishments destroy.

3.

Tho' *Amblerena* spread her snare,
    And caught me in the am'rous vein;
Her vicious soul, her gloating air,
    The thrilling ecstacies restrain.   20
Unhappy females, loosely bold,
    Where southern climates raise desire,
Your faint attractions ne'er will hold,
    Where reason sprinkles but the fire.

4.

Rather let me, where *Gambia* flows,   25
    With black *Fidenia* spend my days,
Than tempt those arms, where lust all glows,
    And mingle with the curs'd embrace.
See! with what majesty she walks!
    What modesty adorns her mien!   30
How simply innocent she talks,
    Inchanting slave! my *Indian* queen!

5.

E'er my exalted, matchless friend
    Had sav'd me from the enrag'd deep,[*]
With what sad cries, thou wail'dst my end,   35
    And how my faithful slave did weep!
How shouts broke forth, with joy replete,

When sav'd, they cast me on the shore!
With rapture, how you hugg'd my feet,
    And all thy gods, how didst implore!   40

6.

For this, I'll grateful, thee convey,
    Where ev'ry precept shall combine,
To chace the savage quite away,
    And all thy motions to refine.
And ev'ry maid, and ev'ry swain,   45
    Shall melt at thy uncommon tale,
With admiration, tell thy name,
    And me, thy happy master, hail!

7.

Nor you, ye fair ones, will condemn
    A grateful mind, for acts like these;   50
Nor such a tenderness arraign,
    Where sense, and wit, and prudence please.
Thou, my *Maria*, shalt embrace
    Fidenia, with a glad surprise;
Hortensia too, her beauties trace,   55
    And own the lustre of her eyes.

                        E. K. v. *G. L. C.*

Title FIDENIA* A very beautiful Negro Girl, aged 16, from *James* River in *Guinea*, who, by every superior Accomplishment, seems far beyond any of her Kind. She learnt the *English* Tongue in three Months Time, and in four, read the *Spectators* and *Tatlers* with inimitable Grace. She has endear'd herself to a grateful Master by her Fidelity and Affection, tho' he has been much censur'd for his Regard to her. (*Kimber's note*)
34   deep,* He was in Danger of drowning in the great Bay of C[hesapeake]; and 'tis impossible to express the tender Concern she show'd, in her Way, on that Occasion. (*Kimber's note*) See *Itinerant Observations*, 58–59.

5

"The Departure"

In terms of subject matter, "The Departure" is the earliest poem associated with Kimber's journey to America. It first appeared in the *London Magazine* (13 [March 1744]: 148; Lemay, *Calendar*, no. 731). The philosophical outlook toward the possibility of losing his life from shipwreck bears little relation to the feelings expressed in *Itinerant Observations*, where shipwreck appears imminent.

The DEPARTURE.

Tune, Farewel to *Lockaber,* &c.

Extempore, over a Bottle, in a Bay, call'd Jack in the Basket, *at the Back of the* Isle of Wight, Sept. 14, 1742, *Wind-bound.*

1.

ADIEU native plains, where blithsome I've rov'd,
Where gayly I've sported, and fondly I've lov'd,
Where friendship's dear charms have enraptur'd my soul,
And wit, sense, and beauty, enliv'ned the bowl:
The precepts of honour now bear me away,   5
And dictates of fortune will force me to stray;
To regions, far distant, prepared to go,
When easterly gales all propitious shall blow.

2.

My dearest relations, and friends, we must part,
But sure, you'll preserve the chief place in my heart;   10
Ye fair ones so tender, so charmingly kind,
Your images ever shall dwell on my mind;
No absence, no distance, shall ever remove
The height of my passion, the strength of my love.
Your worths and your virtues, I'll ever retain,   15
Which, tho't on, will vanquish all grief and all pain.

3.

If powers, fraught with blessings, with wealth crown
    my view,
With how much delight will I share it with you!
If glory and fame should attend on my call,
With what real transport, 'twould gladden you all.   20
But if adverse fate on some barbarous shore,
Should throw my pale coarse, or the waves should devour;
Your sorrow and pity, my death will attend,
Which, e'en in reflection, will soften my end.

E.K. v. *G.L.C.*

6
"Upon Approaching the Coast of New York"

Appearing in the (*London Magazine* 13 [March 1744]: 148; Lemay, *Calendar*, 732), this poem happily mentions *Sandy Hook*, a small spit of land jutting into the sea from the New Jersey coast and a geographic landmark Kimber would reuse in "A Letter from a Son" (lines 95–98).

Written extempore in the Atlantick, *upon approaching the* Coast of New York, *after a six Weeks Voyage from* England.*

PROPITIOUS gale! we hail thy healing power!
Which does our every joyous look restore;
Glads every heart, and brightens every eye,
Whilst former ills are pass'd unheeded by;
Nor storms perplex, nor calms our patience try.   5
Gloomy despair had made e'en *Davis** rave,
And fitted him a subject for the grave:
But cheer'd by thee, his thoughts are blithe and gay;
At once thou chacest all his ills away.
No more nor'westers haunt his troubled mind,   10
But *Sandy Hook's* in every blast of wind.
Ye gladsome shores, appear and bless our fight,
Before are spread the gloomy wings of night.

G.L.C. v. *E.K.*

Title   *after a six Weeks Voyage from* England* See the Song at *New York* in our *Mag.* for *July* last, p. 352. (*Kimber's note*)
  6   *Davis** The most impatient merry Mortal amongst us. (*Kimber's note*)

7
"A Song"

This poem, which first appeared in the *London Magazine* (13 [July 1744]: 358; Lemay, *Calendar*, no. 738), was written at the time of James Oglethorpe's departure from Georgia in July 1743. Though Oglethorpe was returning to England to answer charges brought by Lt. Col. William Cooke and though he had antagonized several influential Savannah residents, he never-theless retained many admirers. By the time Kimber wrote this poem, verse tributes to Oglethorpe had become common-place. *See* Lemay, *Calendar,* nos. 245, 256, 261, 300, 329, 339, 362, 666, 747, 754; and Richard C. Boys, "General Oglethorpe and the Muses," *Georgia Historical Quarterly* 31 (1947): 19–29.

A Song.

In a certain Military Retreat.

Tune, Florimel.

WHAT pleasures more rejoice,
Than those our friendship yields,
And ev'ry moment gilds;
When thus retir'd to envy'd shades,
No anxious care, or pain invades.   5
      Our passions all controul'd,
By reason's op'ning ray,
Which dawns like new-born day;
And ev'ry sentiment refin'd,
Hail! happy we of human kind!   10
      Tho' fleeting from our eyes,
The god-like man[*] departs;
Who sways our honest hearts:
Yet in our souls, his maxims dwell,
Which teach to speak and act so well.   15
      Let fortune fickle frown,
Let adverse fate conspire,
To rob our each desire;
Yet honour's laws we'll still obey,
And follow virtue's glorious way.   20
      M. *and* C.

12 The god-like man[*] The principal Officer was gone to *London.* (*Kimber's note*)

8
"A Letter from a Son"

First published over two issues of the *London Magazine* (13 [July 1744]: 355–57; [August 1744]: 405–6; Lemay, *Calendar,* no. 737), "A Letter from a Son" remains Kimber's most significant poem relating to his American journey. Like *Itinerant Observations*, it retells the story of his trip from his departure from England to his arrival in Georgia. Kimber would quote heavily from this poem in his prose narrative. While Kimber's in medias res organization gives *Itinerant Observations* an epic quality, "A Letter from a Son" achieves its epic quality through the use of blank verse. As Milton had explained in his introduction to *Paradise Lost*, "The measure is *English* heroic Verse without Rime, as that of *Homer* in *Greek*, and of *Virgil* in *Latin;* Rime being no necessary Adjunct or true Ornament of Poem or good Verse, in longer Works especially." Long blank verse epics had achieved considerable popularity in Kimber's day. Richard Glover's *Leonidas*, which Kimber quotes in *Itinerant Observations*, had gone through many editions during the 1730s.

Kimber's tone shifts drastically in the second part. The poem becomes a tearful tribute to his father the poet. The second installment alludes to his mother's insanity, a subject Kimber would later elaborate upon in the eulogistic biographical sketch which prefaced his edition of Isaac Kimber's *Sermons*, where he explained that his father was "visited with a very sore affliction in his Wife's being deprived of her reason ... This malady had two several stages; for some years it displayed itself in ravings and fury, by which his person was often endangered, and then sunk into an indolent kind of frenzy, which continued all the rest of her life" (xiii). The poet ends by promising to return home to remain with his father.

A LETTER *From a* SON, *in a distant Part of the World,*
March 2, 1743.

HAIL, much-lov'd man! forgive the aspiring Muse,
That still, tho' feebly pinion'd, aims to soar;
Whilst I recount my long and wearied course,
From *Albion's* cliffs, to these rough sandy shores.
Supremest Good! whose providential sway,   5
Remotest seas, and prostrate nations tell;
Whether ador'd invisible, all pure,
Diffuse as light, thro'out eternal space;
Or circumscrib'd, a local deity,

As narrow ignorance has long maintain'd;   10
Accept the grateful praise, which, taught to rise
From my glad heart, invades thy open ears,
For ev'ry wonder on my favour wrought,
Whilst roving, thus, thro' ocean's utmost bounds.
      Pleas'd and delighted with the distant scene   15
Of *Asia*'s gorgeous piles, with fleeting haste,
We cross'd to that fam'd town, which, meanly lost,
Caus'd fatal pangs in dying *Mary's* breast.
But there my growing hopes too soon were damp'd,
And mournful, parting from the godlike man,   20
Who snatch'd me from oblivion's sick'ning shade,
I westward bent my solitary way.
Hard circumstance! but what my Lord requests,
What he commands, submiss I still obey.
But ah! my friend, when haply you arrive,   25
Where od'rous gums revive the fragrant air,
Where *Nilus* laves, or sad *Euphrates* rolls;
When gentle zephyrs spread their fanning wings,
Or cooling grottos bar the scorching rays,
Think how I freeze, and how intensly burn;   30
And that must sure provoke the pitying sigh.
      Now *Eurus*, gladsome, fills the swelling sails,
The lab'ring cordage cracks before the wind,
And the sharp prow divides the yielding main.
See, far behind, *Ocrinum's* less'ning height,   35
Known head-land of *Danmonium*, rocky coast,
Long, by the shipwreck'd seaman, justly curs'd:
Now frightful *Scilly* mocks the straining sight,
Whose useful fires, expiring, faintly gleam.
      Adieu, ye native, ever worship'd plains!   40
Yet, 'ere bright *Phoebus*, many annual rounds,
Has with his glorious influence chear'd the globe,
You'll rise, in added splendor, still more bright:
See, pale *Iberians* stricke the obedient flag,
Where e'er thy dreaded fleets triumphant ride;   45
See, humbled *Gaul* with lowly aspect bends,
And asks thy union, with dejected cry!
See ev'ry region of the earth conspire,
To wast their wealth to thy protecting ports!
Ah! may I yet revisit thee once more!   50
Once more survey thy *Thames'* unequalled towers;
Or thro' *Cam's* winding vales, transported stray,

Attentive to *Maria's* moving song.
  Now, afar north, we chill our lifeless blood,
And now, far south, confess the glowing fire,   55
Toss'd and retoss'd from pole to utmost pole;
Whilst storms appale, and calms succeeding teaze.
  Here *Boreas*, blustring o'er the rising waves,
Provokes the horrid storm; see, forked glare
The livid light'nings thro' the vast expanse!   60
And hark! loud thunder rolls with deafning roar!
The black sulphureous clouds discharge their stores,
And the green flashes start the face of night:
No more the helm obeys the pilot's hand;
See, born aloft, our masts pervade the skies,   65
And now we're bury'd in the gulph below.
  Then the scant gale, perplexing, dies away,
Nature is wrapt in hush, and smoothest peace;
And our tall vessel reels her giddy head,
As swell on swell rebuffs her lofty sides.   70
See, azure streaks the crystal vault o'erspread!
Resplendent *Cynthia* gilds the shining deep,
Whose sportive furrows o'er each other play.
  Dreadful vicissitudes! but grateful still,
To minds resolv'd to attain the heights of fame, 75
To genii, who aspire, tho' still surrounded
By ev'ry wretched ill that starts the soul,
To purchase honour, and to serve mankind.
Let reptiles, mean and sordid, safely lurk,
Bury'd luxuriously, in holes and corners;   80
Ours is the useful life, tho' want and anguish,
Famine, and all the direful train of evils,
That human nature shrinks at, oft conspire
To check our frailty in the glorious race.
  Now the thick, foggy mists are seen to rise   85
O'er *Newfoundland's* extensive fishy banks;
And ploughing on with kind auspicious gales,
We pass the false *Nantucket's* treacherous sands;
Till bleak north-westers stop our further course,
Which, fraught with all their wintry plagues, combine, 90
To bar us from our hospitable port.
  At length we view the long'd for, shining spire,
With such a joy as dol'rous mortals feel,
When rais'd from death's approach to lively health:

Scarce we believe or trust our won'dring sight,   95
When *Sandy-Hook* extends its friendly arms,
And the green, verdant spots salute our eyes,
Which, far and wide, the hills and dales o'erspread;
The latest gift of *Ceres* to the year.*
      Fondly I gaze all o'er the seemly pile,   100
And there, my friend, obey'd thy dear commands;
But, tho' my ev'ry gaze invite my stay,
I once again commit me to the waves.
      But sure I well deserv'd the odious name,
Ingratitude conveys, if I not chant   105
Your praises, fair ones of this growing land;
Free, gentle, good, and virtuous, you adorn
The ev'ry stage of life; the duteous child,
Th'endearing mother, and the prudent wife.
This I can tell; but your excelling charms   110
Transcend the reach of my too feeble lay.
Laurentia! ah could I describe thy worth!
For she a *Helen*'s beauty could outvye,
And chaste *Lucretia*'s boasted virtue foil!
How my delighted hours have wing'd their round,   115
Still list'ning as she spoke; for ev'ry grace,
Sure, waited on her tongue and smooth'd her voice.
Adieu, sweet nymph! for ever, nymph, farewel!
No more I see thee guide the whirling wheels,
O'er *Hempstead*'s wide, extended, level plain;   120
Or, wrapp'd in transport, catch thy ev'ry verse,
Soft, tuneful, *Sapho!* gen'rous-hearted fair.
For thee, each year, a festal day shall wake,
To glad me with remembrance of the maid,
And all the joyous hours that she inspir'd!   125
      Alas! my dearest *Campbell*, where are thou?
To echo forth *Laurentia*'s endless praise?
But ah! thou'rt fled, and now exists no more
In mortal semblance! dearest shade, attend!
Ah! hover o'er me with thy angel wings!   130
And chace away the grief that hurts my soul:
Grief, endless grief, for thy untimely fate!
Could rocks and sands, or warring waves conjoin'd,
With howling winds, or all the hideous tribe
Of savages, that prowl this desert waste,   135
Could these and more have wing'd thy latest hour,
We jointly then had render'd up our breath,

Happy to fall united! Now alone
I wander, comfortless, from place to place,
And like the shipwreck'd mariner, aghast,   140
On some curs'd barren shelve, I seek in vain,
With wand'ring eyes, for help in my despair.
        Soon we survey the shores that owe their name
To *Charles*'s bride, high looming from afar;
And soon we change, for all that sailors dread,   145
The spritely music and the sportful dance,
Where jocund damsels, and their well-pleased mates,
Pass the delicious moments, void of care,
And only study how to laugh and love,
Contented, happy, under *Calvert*'s sway.   150
We leave ye, buxom girls, for pathless woods,
And the devouring train that harbour there,
Whose hoarse-ton'd howls, when night has spread her veil,
Terrific shake the hardiest breast with fear.
        But safe, we greet with glad'ned view the Bounds   155
Of that fam'd colony, from whence the weed,
The salutiferous plant, that sends the breast
From noxious vapours of th' inclement morn,
Provocative to solid, studious thought,
Derives its birth and use; the land that erst   160
Employ'd the labours of our virgin queen,
And still is sacred to *Eliza*'s fame.
        Thence far away, the martial trump excites
My active genius to the sanguine field,
T' unsheath my sword upon *Britannia*'s foes,   165
Where southern skies intensly shed their fires,
And all their train of plagues spread far and wide.
The seas obey the ardour of my youth,
And soon I'm wafted to the distant shore;
Where wild *Bellona* dealt her influence round,   170
And wasteful havock reign'd with horrid sway.
        Here must I cease, superior is the theme,
The glorious theme, the great, the godlike chief,
Who rul'd our hosts, and vanquish'd haughty *Spain*,
To my too mean essay. Let *Homer* wake,   175
Let *Virgil* strike once more the sounding string,
Or *Cato*'s better genius* live again;
Their lofty numbers, their aspiring song,
Could only suit the subject of his praise.

Once more, I trust *Neptunian* treach'rous smiles,   180
Asia's grand havens soon will ope' their arms;
Soon will the waving deserts smoke around,
Whose barking monsters gleam all o'er the wild.
But this, ere long, employs prosaic tale;
For 'slant reflection now assaults my heart,   185
And the poetic rapture's spent, expir'd,
Which lent me wings to soar, and voice to sing.
Ye tuneful Nine, ye *Heliconian* fair,
Forgive the fond presumption I express,
In daring, thus, to invocate your names,   190
In this, my latest, this my last offence,
Last profanation of your hallow'd rites:
And happy am I, that my latest song
Pays to my honoured fire the filial due.

[Part 2]

Nil me paeniteat sanum patris hujus: Eoque
Non, ut magna dolo factum negat esse suo pars,
Quod non ingenuos habeat clarosque parentes,
Sic me defendam.———
Hor. Lib. I. Sat. 6.

PARDON, dear Sir, the attemptive, honest verse;   195
For whilst the gloomy, all the dusky train
Of woes, that timid apprehension paints,
(Which, I mistrust, since mournful I retir'd
From *Britain*'s native plains, have vex'd thy soul)
Oppress my sad'ning heart; whilst ev'ry ill,   200
That claims the filial aid, stalks thwart my view;
How can the breathing lyre be taught to sound?
Or, how the swelling note be bid to flow?
Ah! fell ambition, how hast thou misled
My youthful will! vain are thy opening charms,   205
Which, in a blaze of light, attract my steps:
For thee I lost the real, solid good,
Smooth peace, and all those dear paternal precepts,
That still improv'd and brighten'd ev'ry thought;
That chas'd away black error's dreary clouds,   210
With forceful truth's unsully'd, chearing ray;
That aided reason's mild, all-conquering power,
And bar'd each mystic science to my eyes.
Thou best of men and fathers, see the tears,

That long and cruel absence makes me shed!   215
Yes, tho' a *Scythian* roughness speaks my frame,
And *Rome*'s severity has steel'd my breast,
Tho' eagerly I tread each arduous path,
And gladly tempt the rugged front of danger;
Yet, when reflecting on your wond'rous goodness,   220
Your amiable tenderness, the cares
You lavish'd on me, from my infant state
To these more ripen'd years, your silent grief
When fortune forc'd me from you, I dissolve,
And stain my sex with more than female sorrows.   225
For sure, the *Latian* hero, long renown'd,
Who bore his helpless fire, with pious care,
From *Ilium*'s dismal scene; or that fam'd youth,
Sage *Fenelon* so beauteously has sung,
Who long, thro' utmost regions, wand'ring, sought   230
Divine *Ulysses*, ne'er could vie with me,
In fond affection to a reverenc'd parent.
  All that adorns my ever thankful mind,
That humanizes, that with polish'd grace
Directs and mends the heart, I owe to thee;   235
Deep thy dear lessons sunk into my soul,
You bid the form'd ideas move the tongue,
And ev'ry virtue ripen'd in my breast.
  How have we rov'd religion's puz'led maze
In sober, mild debate; till clear'd, illumin'd,   240
Lo!—its dictates shone, freed from the murd'ring hands
Of sightless zeal, and superstition's heat.
Eager, my ears, now catching at the tho't,
Retentive hear you speak, when you diffuse
The saving doctrine, simple, void or art;   245
Which, in mellifluous strains, revives the throng,
And, far and wide, imparts its healing pow'r.
  How dost thou rise in native worth array'd,
When, quite enamour'd in the task, I trace
Thee, thro' the midnight gloom, thou'st tort'ring past!   250
How patient, under all heav'n's dispensations,
You've dragg'd a load of woe, without a sigh!
Heart-wounding woe! unhappiness extreme!
My mother! whilst I utter that lov'd name,
My griefs burst forth, and tears incessant flow.   255
Sempronia ne'er possess'd such moving grace,
Such prudence, and a conduct so refin'd,

With ev'ry winning air that knew to please;
But lost, alas! in dire oblivion drown'd,
Each faculty, that spoke, that long proclaim'd,   260
The fondest parent, and the tend'rest wife!
We view her alter'd frame, with sad regret,
Where baleful frenzy, with its hellish forms,
Romantic revels, all uncouth and wild:
But still her well known beauties, glimmering sport,   265
And, e'en in madness, find a way to charm.
Thanks to the gen'rous seer, whose studious cares,
Whose healing arts, have still preserv'd her life.
Oft I recount her sweet maternal pains,
To plan, with artful speech, the future man: 270
What honied accents danc'd upon her lips!
And how the brighten'd maxims gladsome trill'd!
To bear all this, and more, and be a man,
A patient, a resign'd, a virtuous man,
What kind instructions such examples give!   275
Ye heavens look down! for sure a soul like this,
Deserves your ev'ry bliss, and all your care.
          More pride elates me for thy honest worth,
Than for ought kings or glory could bestow,
Or all the wealth the *Indian* mines contain: 280
And me, propitious fate allots to chear
Thy ev'ry future hour; I'll softly steal
Each comfort to thy heart, with joyous haste,
And ease the burden of oppressive wrong.
As *Egypt's* great preserver sav'd his fire,   285
So will I ev'ry studious way employ,
To wing with pleasure thy remaining days.
See! *Fortune*, fickle goddess, means to smile
Upon my ev'ry path; yet, yet, a while,
And then, I prostrate lowly at thy feet,   290
And empty there, the treasures of the *East*.
Coelestial moments! wing your swift approach!
I glow! I burn! to view my native skies,
To feel myself lock'd in my father's arms.

32 *Eurus* A wind blowing from the eastern parts of the world.
99 *Ceres* The goddess of corn and harvests, frequently identified with
Demeter.
99 year.* In *October*. (*Kimber's note*)
112 *Laurentia!* Kath. Laurence, of New York. *See* above, p. 67.
147–50 Where . . . sway. Kimber would quote these four lines in *The History*

of the Life and Adventures of Mr. Anderson (1754) with the introduction, "Often he [the protagonist, Tom Anderson] would with longing heart think of his beloved Maryland, his innocent Senepuxon" (203).

170 Bellona The goddess of war.

173 godlike chief   James Oglethorpe.

177 Cato's better genius* Addison. (Kimber's note)

188 Heliconian Helicon, the largest mountain of Boeotia, was sacred to the Muses who had a temple there.

Epigraph to part 2   Satires, book 1, line 89–92. Horace, Satires, Epistles and Ars Poetica, translated by H. Rushton Fairclough (1929; Loeb Classical Library, Cambridge: Harvard University Press, 1961), 83: "Never while in my senses could I be ashamed of such a father, and so I will not defend myself, as would a goodly number, who say it is no fault of theirs that they have not free-born and famous parents." Kimber greatly admired Horace, if his later references are any indication. In The History of the Life and Adventures of Mr. Anderson (1754), after the title character has been banished to a distant plantation, a friend brings a pocket edition of Horace, "to alleviate and brighten some of your solitary hours" (84). A few pages later, he could be found "retired into his cot, with his Horace, and pleasing himself with the fine conceptions of that elegant poet" (90).

9
"A Ballad"

This playful poem appeared in the London Magazine (13 [August 1744]: 406–7. Lemay, Calendar, no. 740). Here, Kimber good-heartedly juxtaposes the valor of his own regiment with that of another group of soldiers, possibly a neighboring Carolina regiment. The toast to the "great CHIEF" refers to Oglethorpe.

A BALLAD.

Occasion'd by some Attempts of a certain Colony, to be witty on a neighbouring Corps of brave Gentlemen, by calling them BOYS.

————Risum teneatis Amici
Sic cecinere B.D.W.G.M.M.H.M.M.O.B.W.C.

1.

I'LL tell you, good sirs, what will make you all smile,
Enliven the glass, and the time will beguile,

That whilst each true heart here his comrade enjoys,
We are all stigmatiz'd by the term of the *boys*.

　　　　　　　　　　　　　　　　Derry down, &c.

2.

But 'faith, tho' it seems to affront us all round,　　5
Its malignity only consists in the sound;
For if you'll examine the world's constant story,
They were *boys*, much like us, that have shar'd all its glory.

3.

Alexander and *Caesar*, and hundreds beside,
Whose acts are our G————'s pattern and pride,　　10
And the fam'd dirty Swede, all our hist'ries agree,
Were all, to a man, just as *boyish* as we.

4.

If states have been rais'd, and if laws have been made,
And if sciences taught, arts encourag'd, and trade;
As a serious truth I affirm and assure ye,　　15
The plans were all laid by such souls as are near ye.

5.

And pray ye, let's pause, and examine the times,
That have giv'n us our births, and this chorus of rhymes,
And you'll find most of those, who are trump'd out by fame,
To be just such brave *boys*, and to laud the gay name.　　20

6.

But let us explain, ye damn'd critical fops,
Who carp at a sentence before e'en it drops,
To silence your snarling, and stop your dull noise,
Why 'tis that we're pleas'd with the term of the *boys*.

7.

The term, to be sure, bears a trifling sense,　　25
But this we alledge in the culprit's defence,
That because it is modest, so highly we prize it;
For we're willing to own, we are not wholly wise yet.

8.

Now ye sour-fac'd, splenetic, deep politic's wretches,

What, what will become of your schemes and your   30
    fetches,
When *boys* thus united your wrath can provoke,
And scatter your wisdom as wind scatters smoak?

9.

    Ah! how must you dread our approach of ripe age,
When experience, with years, shall adorn ev'ry sage;
If our juvenile knowledge makes such a curs'd pother,   35
And causes such pangs in each long-headed brother?

10.

    I think we've convinc'd the grave long-whisker'd foe,
That they dealt with brave *boys*, not a long while ago;
And we hope soon to hear that gay capering *France*,*
Will give us occasion to lead 'em a dance.   40

11.

    My fancy transports me to *E*———'s fair scene,
Where our G———haply may one day be seen,
All gloriously great with his sons on the plain,
To prove even there that his *boys* are all men.

12.

    And let vagabond tr—sp—ts from hence ever cease 45
To be fancy, but wear their umbrellas in peace;
For their impotent malice provokes but our smiles,
Whilst we hamper their projects, and puzzle their wiles.

13.

    All social in mirth, and for ever united,
Still charm'd with each other, and always delighted;   50
We talk and we jest, and we laugh and we sing,
And with our whole hearts hail our G— and KING.

14.

    Then fill up the bumpers, come, come, fill along,
For an excellent toast shall finish our song;
And let's all together extend high the voice,   55
So here's our great CHIEF and his ne'er conquer'd *boys*.

39 *France,** This was just before we heard of the *French* War. (*Kimber's note*)

10
"The Repentant Deboshee"

London Magazine (13 [August 1744]: 408; Lemay, *Calendar*, no. 741). While so many of the other poems are autobiographical, this misogynistic poem appears to be a deliberate fiction, though it does express similar ideas as "The Vindication." Kimber's speaker styles himself "Fidelio," a man whose changeable affections shifted from one woman to another with nothing but heartbreak and dissatisfaction. By the end of the poem, Fidelio resolves to abandon his amorous pursuits and pursue reason.

The REPENTANT DEBOSHEE.

——Nocet empta dolore voluptas.
HOR.

ALAS! whilst aching pains declare
The wretched courses I have run,
Let ev'ry friend avoid the snare,
    That tolls *Fidelio* he's undone,
The wand'ring fires that still destroy   5
Each taste of life, each glimpse of joy.
Involv'd in guilt's most deadly sty,
    Prostrate, supine, oppress'd with woe,
Scarce can the lamp of life supply
    Repentant tears, that fain would flow: 10
Repentant tears, ah! shed too late,
To ease my mind, or change my fate.
Curs'd be the fair, who first allur'd,
    And all my poison'd juices fir'd;
And thou, in midnight gloom obscur'd,   15
    And thou, ah! *P*——*t,* so much admir'd:
Ungrateful traitress! thus to wound,
And cast thy baleful darts around.
Once jetty Black engag'd my vows,
    And then the tawny *F*——*s* came,   20
Till *W*——*h,* to whom all *G*—— bows,
    Eclips'd the well-experienc'd dame:
Where now the rapt'rous joyous scene?
Haste, can you hide me from my sin.

Ah! prudent *H*———*s*, lovely maid,   25
    Could thy dear charms have fix'd my heart,
Or *A*———*n*'s flowing sense persuade
    A wretch, such vices to desert,
No tort'ring tho'ts would rend my breast,
Of murd'ring lust, or nymphs distrest.   30
Ye false, ye fascinating crew,
    Replete with strange bewitching wiles,
Hence! hence! I ever bid adieu
    To all your fell, destructive smiles:
From me for ever be remov'd,   35
The baneful haunts, so oft I've rov'd.
All restless, tossing too and fro,
    Now here, now there, my tortures rage;
And wakeful conscience shocking throws,
    No hopes can heal, no arts assuage.   40
Supreme look down, and hear my pray'r,
And let they mercy cure dispair.
I see, I see thy goodness dawn,
    And gleam o'er my reviving soul;
As dews, the parch'd-up funny lawn,   45
    It chears the pangs that inly roul.
Gladsome, I trace the fields of day,
Whilst op'ning reason leads the way.

                                    INDICUS.

Epigraph Epistulae, book 1, epistle 2, line 55. Horace, *Satires, Epistles and Ars Poetica*, 267: "Pleasure bought with pain is harmful."

11

"Acrostic"

    The first letter of each line of this poem (*London Magazine* 13 [August 1744]: 408. Lemay, *Calendar*, no. 742) spells "Susanna Anne L. K." With the final "K," Kimber anticipates his marriage to Susanna Lunn. The poem's content is fairly conventional. More interesting is the pseudonym, "Peregrinus Vespusianus," a name that reflects Kimber's growing sense of himself as a traveler and his emerging identification with America.

ACROSTIC.

S oft as the downy plumage of the dove,
U number'd graces o'er her features rove.
S uch was the fair, whom *Paris* made his prize;
A h! had she had thy virtues with thy eyes,
N ever had valiant *Hector* then expir'd,
N or *Troy*'s bright domes revengeful wrath had fir'd,
A nd ev'ry future age had still admir'd.

A nd see the nymph, in whom all sweetness shines,
N *ancy*, whom prudence and whom wit refines;
N o gloom obscures her ever glad'ning smiles,
E ach sense the charms, and ev'ry care beguiles.

L ong may the maids, in virtue's rules secure,
K eep still united, innocent, and pure.

PEREGRINUS VESPUSIANUS.

12
"On Making Foul-Island"

London Magazine (13 [September 1944]: 461). According to Kimber's manuscript itinerary, he saw Foul Island on 7 June 1744. This playful quatrain shows that, despite the rough passage, Kimber retained his sense of humor. He even carried his humor into the footnote.

On making Foul-Island, *after a bad Voyage, North about, from* Charles-Town, South-Carolina, *to* England.

FOUL winds, foul weather vex'd us fore,
    And foul'd with grief each blithsome soul;
With fouler luck to vex us more,
    The very land we make is *Foul.*

---

4 *Foul.** However, to do Justice, 'tis no bad Landfall, though we thought to make Fair-Isle. (*Kimber's note*)

13
"Written Extempore in the Castle of Edinburgh"

This poem, which appeared in the *London Magazine* (13 [September 1744]: 461), provides details not in *Itinerant Observations*. While the poem's long title states that Kimber had reaching Edinburgh by 9 June 1744, his manuscript itinerary states that he "arrived at Leith, near Edinburgh, after beating 3 days in the Frith of Forth, June 15." Lines 3–4 may be a tribute to the Highlanders who settled at Darien, Georgia.

Written extempore in the Castle of Edinburgh,
June 9, 1744.

WINDSOR, no more thy chearing views invite.
What joyful prospects glad my straining sight!
Hail, *Scotia's* sons, who restless ever roam,
Far from your native skies, delightful home:
Ill you requite the providential care,   5
That bless'd your land, with all that's great and fair.
What distant scenes of golden plenty rise,
What hills and dales and glitt'ring domes surprise,
And gaily charm each fond beholder's eyes!
See gaudy *Fife's* eternal towered sides,   10
'Gainst which the *Friths*, tumultuous roll their tides.
Well might the merry monarch* call the land,
Whose num'rous towns enliven all the strand,
And all around the blithsome shire embrace,
A velvet cloak fu' richly edg'd with lace.   15
Yon reverend town,* whose ev'ry lofty spire,
And antique fabrics sacred awe inspire,
The seat of royal kings, a lengthen'd line,
Tho' with a faded lustre, still does shine.
Where ere I turn me to the magic round,   20
Ten thousand various wonders still are found.
Let malice own, that long with carping tongue
Has scorn'd thy charms, with baleful envy stung,
Thy beauties, so despis'd, are past compare;
Thy men all valiant, and thy women fair.   25
Ah! tho' oppress'd, let ev'ry nation see
Thy patriot sons unbias'd, hold and free.

         P. V. C. ANGLICUS.

12 monarch* James I. (*Kimber's note*)
16 town,* Edinburgh. (*Kimber's note*)

14
"Written on a Brick"

The date of this poem, which appeared in the *London Maga-zine* (13 [September 1744]: 461), also differs from that in the manuscript itinerary, where Kimber wrote that he was "forced to put into Holy Island, June 23."

Written on a Brick, in the Ruins of HOLY-ABBEY, *on* HOLY-ISLAND, *near,* Berwick on Tweed, *June* 21, 1744.

YE gloomy vaults, ye hoary cells,
    Ye cloyster'd domes, in ruin great,
Where sad and mournful silence dwells,
    How well instruct ye by your fate?

Thus ev'ry human pride and boast   5
    Shall soon or later meet decay;
In dark oblivion sunk and lost,
    The idle pageants of a day.

Ah! what is life! a passing hour!
    A fleeting dream of fancy'd joy!   10
No constant blessing in our power,
    But dullest repetitions cloy.

How frail, how weak is human art,
    By works like these, to raise a name!
What empty vapours swell the heart!   15
    On what strange plans we build for fame!

'Tis virtue only laughs at age,
    And soars beyond the reach of time,
Mocks at the tyrant's fiercest rage,
    For ever awfully sublime.   20
                  P. V. C.

Notes

Introduction

1. For biographical information on Isaac Kimber, see *DNB;* Edward Kimber, "Memoirs of the Life and Writings of the Reverend Mr. Isaac Kimber," in Isaac Kimber, *Sermons on the Most Interesting Religious, Moral, and Practical Subjects* (London: C. and J. Ackers, 1756), i–xvii; Sidney A. Kimber, "The 'Relation of a Late Expedition to St. Augustine,' with Biographical and Bibliographical Notes on Isaac and Edward Kimber," *PBSA* 28 (1934): 81–96 (hereinafter, "Biographical Notes").

2. J. A. Leo Lemay, *Men of Letters in Colonial Maryland* (Knoxville: University of Tennessee Press, 1972), 363; Lemay, *A Calendar of American Poetry in the Colonial Newspapers and Magazines and in the Major English Magazines Through 1765* (Worcester: American Antiquarian Society, 1972), nos. 252A, 258.

3. For a list of Kimber's contributions to the *London Magazine* through 1758, *see The General Index to Twenty-Seven Volumes of the London Magazine; viz. from 1732 to 1758 Inclusive* (London: R. Baldwin, 1760).

4. *London Magazine* 11 (May 1742): 248.

5. In the manuscript notebook, Kimber wrote, "Embkd at Grvsnd, in the Br. Grffths, for New York Sept. 11. 1742. arrived there Nov. 1." This and other key passages from the notebook are reprinted in Sidney A. Kimber, "Biographical Notes," 82–83.

6. Manuscript notebook: "Embd. in the Nightingale. Sloop, Newbould, Nov. 13, 1742"; Sidney A. Kimber, "Biographical Notes," 82.

7. *Intellectual Life in the Colonial South, 1585–1763* (Knoxville: University of Tennessee Press, 1978), 3:1435.

8. Manuscript notebook: "Travelled thro' Golden Quarter, Acomoco, Worcester & Northamptonshires, & crossd the Bay of Chesapeak, from Magidi Bay, & arrivd at York, in Virginia, Nov. 25"; Sidney A. Kimber, "Biographical Notes," 82.

9. Manuscript notebook: "Embrkd there [Yorktown], in the Sloop, Bradley, Lucas, for Grga, Dec. 23, & arriv'd in St. Simon's Harbour, Jan. 7. 1742"; Sidney A. Kimber, "Biographical Notes," 83.

10. Quoted in Sidney A. Kimber, introduction to Edward Kimber, *A Relation or Journal of a Late Expedition to the Gates of St. Augustine on Florida* (Boston: Charles E. Goodspeed & Co., 1935), vii.

11. *A Relation, or Journal of a Late Expedition*, ed. John Jay Tepaske (Gainesville: University Press of Florida, 1976), 24.

12. Frank Gees Black, "Edward Kimber: Anonymous Novelist of the Mid-Eighteenth Century," *Harvard Studies and Notes in Philology and Literature* 17 (1935): 36.

13. Manuscript notebook: "Left Frdrca, in the Cutter, Mar. 23, 1744, arrived at the Darien, the same night, & at Wormsloe Mar. 29. Next day visited

Savannah, & arriv'd at Fort Frederick, near Beaufort, in South Carolina, in the Scout boat, Apr. 5. Departed from Beaufort, on Port Royal Island, the next day, by land, & arriv'd at Charles Town Apr. 10"; Sidney A. Kimber, "Biographical Notes," 83.

14. Manuscript notebook: "Embarkd there [Charleston] in the Two Sisters, Stedman, bound for Cowes & Rotterdam, on Apr. 20, & on May 2, our Capt. reslved to go north about, which we did, in company with the Rachael, Perkins, & the . . . Cox. Saw Foula June 7, made the Orkneys & Shetland 2 days after, & arrived at Leith, near Edinburgh, after beating 3 days in the Frith of Forth, June 15.—Set sail from Leith in the sloop Cuthbert, Whitby, for Newcastle, June 21; but were forced to put into Holy Island, June 23. On the 24th took passage in the smack, Loyalty, for Gravesend, and arrivd at Holy Haven, July 1, 1744. The next day sailed in a wherry for Gravesend, & from thence, next day, in the Tilt-boat, for London"; Sidney A. Kimber, "Biographical Notes," 83.

15. "To the Author of the London Magazine," *London Magazine* 13 (September 1744): 444–46; "Parallel between the Late Earl of Peterborough and General Oglethorpe," *London Magazine* 13 (November 1744): 541–46.

16. *A Relation*, 7.

17. *London Magazine* 15 (December 1746): 623–24.

18. From 1755 through 1758 there appeared within the pages of the *London Magazine* a series of essays titled "A Short Account of the British Plantations in America." In *Captain John Smith: A Reference Guide* (Boston: G.K. Hall, 1991), 9, I assigned the work to Kimber, but in Kimber's own *General Index to . . . the London Magazine*, he does not mention his authorship of the series. This is not to say that he did not write it. To be sure, there are other items which he wrote for the *London Magazine* that he does not give himself credit for in the index. Still, I am more hesitant to attribute "A Short Account" to him now than I was when I compiled the Smith bibliography.

19. John Alden and Dennis C. Landis, eds., *European Americana: A Chronological Guide to Works Printed in Europe Relating to the Americas, 1493–1776* (New York: Readex Books, 1982–   ), nos. 750/177, 750/178.

20. W. Gordon Milne, "A Glimpse of Colonial America As Seen in an English Novel of 1754," *Maryland Historical Magazine* 42 (1947): 239–52.

21. Black, "Edward Kimber: Anonymous Novelist," 28.

22. Sidney A. Kimber, "Biographical Notes," 89–90.

23. Quoted in *DNB*.

24. *National Union Catalog: Pre-1956 Imprints* (hereinafter, *NUC*), 754 vols. (London: Mansell, 1968–1981), no. L0290901.

25. *NUC*, no. T0304532.

26. The date assigned is Kimber's own. *NUC* lists no 1760 edition of the work.

27. *NUC*, no. L0019401. Copies of *The Ladies Complete Letter-Writer* could be found throughout colonial America. *See*, for example, *A Catalogue of Mein's Circulating Library* (Boston: [McAlpine and Fleeming,] 1765), 36; *A Catalogue of a Very Large Assortment of . . . Books . . . Which Are to Be Sold by Cox & Berry at Their Store in King-Street, Boston* ([Boston, 1772?]), 3; "Daybook for 1764–1766," in *Virginia Gazette Daybooks 1750–1752 & 1764–1766*, ed., Paul P. Hoffman, (University of Virginia Library: Microfilm Publications, 1967), fols. 8, 25, 41, 140. For a discussion of *The Ladies Complete*

Letter-Writer, see Kevin J. Hayes, *A Colonial Woman's Bookshelf* (Knoxville: University of Tennessee Press, 1996), 73–75.

28. *Monthly Review* 30 (1764): 243. The Bodleian copy was filmed as part of the "English Literary Periodicals" microfilm series.

29. *Critical Review* 6 (1758): 261.

30. *Critical Review* 2 (1756): 379. For a listing of the contemporary reviews of Kimber's novel, *see* Antonia Forster, *Index to Book Reviews in England, 1749–1774* (Carbondale and Edwardsville: Southern Illinois University Press, 1990), 165–66.

31. S. John Roscoe, *John Newberry and His Successors, 1740–1814: A Bibliography* (Wormley, England: Five Owls Press, 1973), no. J211.

32. Research Libraries Information Network (RLIN), no. NYPX92-B4213.

33. Robert Watt, *Bibliotheca Britannica; Or A General Index to British and Foreign Literature* (Edinburgh: for Archibald Constable, 1824), 2:570.

34. S. Austin Allibone, *A Critical Dictionary of English Literature and British and American Authors,* (Philadelphia: J. B. Lippincott, 1870), 2:1030.

35. James Kennedy, W. A. Smith, and A. F. Johnson, *Dictionary of Anonymous and Pseudonymous English Literature (Samuel Halkett and John Laing)* (Edinburgh and London: Oliver and Boyd, 1926–1934), 4:319; Dennis E. Rhodes and Anna E. C. Simoni, *Dictionary of Anonymous and Pseudonymous English Literature (Samuel Halkett and John Laing): Addenda to Volumes I–VIII* (Edinburgh and London: Oliver and Boyd, 1962).

36. *Collections* 4 (1878), part 2. *Itinerant Observations in America. Reprinted from the London Magazine, 1745–6* (Savannah: J. H. Estill, 1878).

37. "The English Colonization of Georgia," in *Narrative and Critical History of America,* ed. Justin Winsor (Boston: Houghton, Mifflin, 1887), 5:401.

38. The selection from *Itinerant Observations* appeared in two installments as "Observations in Several Voyages and Travels in America," *William and Mary College Quarterly* 15 (January 1907): 143–59; and "Observations in Several Voyages and Travels in America in the Year 1736," *William and Mary College Quarterly* 15 (April 1907): 215–25. Further complicating matters, the January installment (at least the copy I examined) was mispaginated (pages 1–17 for 143–59) and misnumbered (volume 16 for 15). Furthermore the April installment parenthetically notes that it is "From *The London Magazine,* July, 1746," but the selection it reprints comes from the November and December 1746 issues of the *London Magazine.* For an example of a scholar led astray by the mistaken 1736 date, *see* Edward M. Riley's otherwise authoritative treatments of Yorktown architecture, "The Colonial Courthouses of York County, Virginia," *William and Mary Quarterly,* 2d ser., 22 (1942): 399–414; and "The Ordinaries of Colonial Yorktown." *William and Mary Quarterly,* 2d ser., 23 (1943): 8–23.

39. Leonard L. MacKall, "The Wymberley Jones De Renne Georgia Library," *Georgia Historical Quarterly* 2 (June 1918): 71.

40. "Views of Yorktown and Gloucester Town, 1755," *Virginia Magazine of History and Biography* 54 (April 1946): 101. Two issues later, Swem acknowledged Kimber's authorship. *See* "Notes and Queries," *Virginia Magazine of History and Biography* 54 (October 1946): 344.

41. *Travels in the Old South: A Bibliography,* vol. 1 (Norman: University of Oklahoma Press, 1956), no. 109.

42. Gregory A. Stiverson and Patrick H. Butler, III, "Virginia in 1732:

The Travel Journal of William Hugh Grove," *Virginia Magazine of History and Biography* 85 (January 1977): 22, note 14.

43. E. Merton Coulter, *Wormsloe: Two Centuries of a Georgia Family* (Athens: University of Georgia Press, 1955), 20.

44. William M. Kelso, *Captain Jones's Wormslow: A Historical, Archaeological, and Architectural Study of an Eighteenth-Century Plantation Site near Savannah, Georgia* (Athens: University of Georgia Press, 1979), 6.

45. "Eighteenth Century Maryland as Portrayed in the 'Itinerant Observations' of Edward Kimber," *Maryland Historical Magazine* 51 (1956): 315–36.

46. Davis, *Intellectual Life in the Colonial South* (1978), 3:1714, notes that an edition of *Itinerant Observations* had been published by the Beehive Press in Savannah in 1975, but Davis's note was premature. The Beehive edition of *Itinerant Observations* never appeared.

47. Lemay, "The Frontiersman from Lout to Hero: Notes on the Significance of the Comparative Method and the Stage Theory in Early American Literature and Culture," *Proceedings of the American Antiquarian Society* 88 (1978): 187–223; Dell Upton, "White and Black Landscapes in Eighteenth-Century Virginia," *Places: A Quarterly Journal of Environmental Design* 2, no. 2 (1985): 59–72; Carson Cary, Norman F. Barka, William M. Kelso, Garry Wheeler Stone, and Dell Upton, "Impermanent Architecture in the Southern American Colonies," *Winterthur Portfolio* 16 (1981); Allan Kulikoff, "The Origins of Afro-American Society in Tidewater Maryland and Virginia, 1700 to 1790," *William and Mary Quarterly*, 3d ser., 35 (1978): 236; Peter E. Martin, "Williamsburg: The Role of the Garden in 'Making a Town,'" *Studies in Eighteenth-Century Culture* 12 (1983): 187–204; and Anne Elizabeth Yentsch, *A Chesapeake Family and Their Slaves: A Study in Historical Archaeology* (New York: Cambridge University Press, 1994), 19, 372.

48. For the best treatment of such language, *see* John Arthos, *The Language of Natural Description in Eighteenth-Century Poetry* (1949; reprint, New York: Octagon Books, 1966).

49. Davis, *Intellectual Life in the Colonial South*, 1:65, first made this observation.

Itinerant Observations in America

1. James Oglethorpe established Fort Frederica in 1736, naming it in honor of Frederick Louis, the Prince of Wales and only son of King George II. A small temporary fort was quickly replaced by a solid fortification, the most costly fort the British had then established in America. Behind the fort, Oglethorpe built the town of Frederica, and each soldier received a sixty- by ninety-foot lot. Kimber's detailed description of Frederica contributes much to our knowledge of the fort and the town. For a thorough treatment of the fort, *see* Albert C. Manucy, *The Fort at Frederica*, vol. 5 of the Department of Anthropology Notes in Anthropology (Tallahassee: Florida State University, 1962). *See also* Trevor R. Reese, *Frederica, Colonial Fort and Town* (St. Simons Island, Ga.: Fort Frederica Association, 1969); and Charles C. Jones, Jr., *The Dead Towns of Georgia* (1878; reprint, Spartanburg, S.C.: Reprint Co., 1974).

The name of the Altamaha River is a corruption of Altama or the Indian for "the way to Tama Country." Tama was an Indian village located at the point where the Oconee and Ocmulgee rivers flow together to form the Altamaha; Margaret Davis Cate, *Our Yesterdays and Todays: A Story of Brunswick and the Coastal Islands*, rev. ed. (Brunswick, Georgia: Glover Bros., 1930), 207–8; Willard Neal, "Altamaha," *Georgia Rivers*, ed. George Hatcher (Athens: University of Georgia Press, 1962), 24–25. Kimber calls the river famous because the Spanish forces sailed through Jekyl Sound (also known as St. Simons Sound) and up the Altamaha during their invasion of Georgia.

2. A Mixture of Lime, made of Oyster-Shells, with Sand, small Shells, &c. which, when harden'd, is as firm as Stone. I have observ'd prodigious Quantities of Salt Petre to issue from Walls of this Cement. (*Kimber's note*) Kimber's use of the word tappy or, as it has come to be spelled, tabby, antedates the usages listed in the *Dictionary of American English* and the *Dictionary of Americanisms*, which both cite a 1775 South Carolina account, and the *Oxford English Dictionary*, which cites an 1802 Georgia account. The *Dictionary of Americanisms* explains that the word is chiefly confined to the Gullah region along the coast of Georgia and South Carolina and was probably brought to the area from African slaves who derived it from the Arabic "tabix," meaning cement, mortar, or brick. For further information on the uses of tabby at Fort Frederica, *see* Margaret Davis Cate, *Early Days of Coastal Georgia* (St. Simons Island, Georgia: Fort Frederica Association, 1955), 25.

3. See *Lond. Mag.* 1742, p. 461, 515, 516, 567. (*Kimber's note*) These reports appeared in the "Monthly Chronologer" portion of the *London Magazine* for September, October, and November, 1742. Isaac Kimber had taken them from reports originally published in the *London Gazette*. They might have been written by Patrick Sutherland, a member of Oglethorpe's regiment. Sutherland returned to London in late 1742, and a full report of the Spanish invasion by him appeared in the *London Gazette*, 25 December 1742. Sutherland's report was separately published as *An Account of the Late Invasion of Georgia* (London, 1743); Thomas D. Clark, *Travels in the Old South: A Bibliography* (Norman: University of Oklahoma Press, 1956), no. 160. For the best modern treatment, see Margaret D. Cate, "Fort Frederica and the Battle of Bloody Marsh," *Georgia Historical Quarterly* 27 (June 1943): 111–74.

4. Shingles are split out of many Sorts of Wood, in the Shape of Tiles, which, when they have been some Time expos'd to the Weather, appear of the Colour of Slate, and have a very pretty Look; the Houses in *America* are mostly shingled. (*Kimber's note*)

5. See *Lond. Mag.* 1744, p. 359. (*Kimber's note*) The brief account appeared as a news item in "The Monthly Chronologer." Though the explosion took place on 22 March 1743/44, the report is dated "*Frederica in Georgia*, March 29." Kimber left Frederica on 23 March 1743/44, the day after the explosion, so the account was probably not written by him. Perhaps Kimber encouraged a friend at Frederica to send newsworthy reports to Isaac Kimber in London. Here follows the complete account: "On the 22d Instant our largest Bomb Magazine, and also a smaller one of Powder, which stood at a considerable Distance from the other, were both set on fire, and blown up, no body knows how, or by whom; but it is shrewdly suspected, that this Piece of Villainy was perpetrated by an *Irishman*, set on by the *Spaniards*, who came down lately to this Place from *Charles-Town*, but disappeared the next Morning after it happened. The Corporal of the Guard, with two Centi-

nels, have been examined, and are still under Confinement, in order for Trial; many Houses are damaged by the Splinters of the Bombs, and some burnt; but the Magazine at the Fort, and the two other lesser ones, full of Bombs and Powder are safe. It seems very extraordinary, that no body received any Hurt on this Occasion, except one Centinel, who was wounded only in the Arm"; *London Magazine* 13 (July 1744): 359.

6. I have been told that in this Explosion, near 3000 Bombs burst, which, had they not been well bedded, would have done much Mischief. (*Kimber's note*)

7. In order to connect Fort Frederica with Fort St. Simons at the island's southeastern point, Oglethorpe decided to make a road upon which soldiers could walk two abreast. The road was begun and completed during the last week of September 1728. Through the marshy areas, Oglethorpe's workmen constructed wooden causeways. Cate, *Early Days of Coastal Georgia*, 31.

8. Captain Raymond Demere (d. 1766), a French Huguenot who had come to Georgia in 1736 with Oglethorpe, was commissioned to be a lieutenant in Oglethorpe's regiment on 25 August 1737, promoted to the position of Captain Lieutenant to Oglethorpe's own company on 12 May 1741, and further promoted on 31 January 1742; W. R. Williams, "British-American Officers, 1720 to 1763," *South Carolina Historical and Genealogical Magazine* 33 (1932): 188, 191. Demere named his home Harrington Hall in honor of Lord Harrington under whom he had served at Gibraltar; Cate, *Our Todays and Yesterdays*, 69–72; Cate, *Early Days of Coastal Georgia*, 226. In 1745, William Logan described Demere's plantation as "ab^t. 1½ mile from Town, a very poor flat sandy spot, but stocked with Young Trees, as Peaches, Apples, Oranges, Pomegrannet &c."; "William Logan's Journal of a Journey to Georgia, 1745," *Pennsylvania Magazine of History and Biography* 36 (1912): 171.

9. Dr. Thomas Hawkins, surgeon to Oglethorpe's Regiment, lived in one of Frederica's finest houses; Margaret Davis Cate, "The Original Houses of Frederica, Georgia: The Hawkins-Davison Houses," *Georgia Historical Quarterly* 40 (1956): 203–12. By Hawkins's plantation Kimber means the three-hundred-acre grant that Hawkins obtained along with William Horton, Willes Weston, and Thomas Hird ostensibly for the maintenance of the Anglican cleric on St. Simons Island; Kenneth Coleman, *Entry Books of Commissions, Powers, Instructions, Leases, Grants of Land, Etc. by the Trustees*, vol. 32 of *The Colonial Records of the State of Georgia* (Athens: University of Georgia Press, 1989), 269–71.

10. Oglethorpe's home, a modest one and a half story tabby cottage that measured about sixteen by thirty-two feet, was located on a three-hundred-acre tract known to Oglethorpe's contemporaries as "The Farm"; Cate, *Early Days of Coastal Georgia*, 35; M. H. and D. B. Floyd, "Oglethorpe's Home at Frederica," *Georgia Historical Quarterly* 20 (1936): 245. M. H. and D. B. Floyd conjecture that Oglethorpe's home "appears never to have been intended by him as his permanent home; but to serve as an encouragement for his soldier-settlers, both by him setting the example and by placing before their eyes a model frontier home and farm" (247). Kimber's description helps validate the conjecture.

11. In 1736 Oglethorpe had attempted to land the third transport of the religious exiles from Salzburg, but they insisted upon going to Ebenezer, Georgia to join their fellow Salzburgers. Most of the residents at German Village on St. Simons Island were not technically Salzburgers. While

Kimber was at Frederica, the German Village received its first pastor, Johann Ulrich Driessler, who, according to Johann Martin Boltzius, began ministering to a congregation of sixty-two souls. George Fenwick Jones, *The Georgia Dutch: From the Rhine and Danube to the Savannah, 1733–1783* (Athens: University of Georgia Press, 1992), 42–43, 57–67.

12. Larry E. Ivers explains: "Lieutenant Robert Scroggs and about six men of his Troop of English Rangers established a camp approximately four miles northwest of Frederica on the mainland. The location, called White Post, or Carteret's Point, at the head of Grant Creek, guarded the land approach to Frederica. Scroggs constructed a small fortification there named Bachelor's Redoubt, which was probably a blockhouse inside a small square stockade"; *British Drums on the Southern Frontier* (Chapel Hill: University of North Carolina Press, 1974), 137.

13. Albert Desbrisay (d. 1742) was commissioned as captain lieutenant to Oglethorpe's Regiment on 25 August 1737; Williams, *British-American Officers*, 188. He had a plantation at West Point; Cate, *Early Days of Coastal Georgia*, 225. Desbrisay is probably most well known for the duel in which he stabbed and killed Captain Richard Norbury; Thomas Gamble, *Savannah Duels and Duellists, 1733–1877* (Savannah: Review Publishing, 1923), 2–3.

14. Cate explains: "South of Hampton, on Frederica River 'from whence they can see vessels a great way to the Northward,' Oglethorpe set up a 'Watch House' in charge of Richard Pike, one of the indentured servants who had been maimed in the public service. Pike and his wife, the daughter of a freeholder at Frederica, lived on this site which became known as Pike's Bluff. A corporal's guard was stationed there and the soldiers were rotated weekly"; *Early Days of Coastal Georgia*, 225.

15. Captain George Dunbar's plantation was located on the bank of Dunbar Creek; Cate, *Early Days of Coastal Georgia*, 226.

16. The Inhabitants begin to plant this charming Fruit very much, and, 'tis to be hop'd, will banish their numerous Peach Trees to their Country Settlements, which are Nurseries of Muskettos, and other Vermin. The Season I was there, they had Oranges enough of their own Growth for Home Consumption. (*Kimber's note*)

17. In *The History of the Life and Adventures of Mr. Anderson* (1754; reprint, New York: Garland, 1975), Kimber would describe the palmetto as "A shrub with large, fanlike, leaf, with which in *America*, huts and cabins are cover'd, or thatch'd" (106n).

18. The bailiffs or magistrates were the chief officials of the colony and judges of its court, and the recorder was another official appointed to the court. The town was divided into tithings, and each tithingman was in charge of the ten men under him when they stood guard. Constables oversaw wards, a larger geographic division which included numerous tithings. Kenneth Coleman, *Colonial Georgia: A History* (New York: Charles Scribner's Sons, 1976), 29, 91.

19. This was written in the Beginning of 1743. (*Kimber's note*)

20. *Aeneid*, book 1, line 204. Virgil, *Eclogues, Georgics, Aeneid I–IV*, trans. H. Rushton Fairclough (1916; rev. ed., Loeb Classical Library, Cambridge: Harvard University Press, 1947), 255: "Through divers mishaps, through so many perilous chances."

21. It very much surpriz'd me to see such an incredible Quantity of Purslain grow amongst the Foundations of the Houses, for I never saw so much

any where else. It should seem that Lime and Shells were a very proper Bed for it. (*Kimber's note*)

22. As at *Porto Bello, Chagre,* and even before, at the Siege of St. *Augustine.* (*Kimber's note*) British forces, under the command of Vice-Admiral Edward Vernon, took Portobello and Chagre in late 1739 and early 1740 and destroyed the Spanish fortifications at each location; Richard Pares, *War and Trade in the West Indies, 1739–1763* (1936; London: Frank Cass, 1963), 110–11.

23. When Oglethorpe first settled St. Simons Island, he sent Lieutenant Philip Donegal to the southeast point of the island to establish a fort which could oversee the entrance into the harbor. The earthen fort, known as Fort Donegal, was replaced by the larger and stronger fortification known as Fort St. Simons after Oglethorpe's return from England in 1738. During the Spanish invasion of Georgia in 1742, the fort was unable to prevent the Spanish from entering the harbor. On 5 July they entered St. Simons Sound. Oglethorpe abandoned the fort to concentrate his forces at Fort Frederica, and the Spanish took possession of Fort St. Simons. Cate, *Early Days of Coastal Georgia,* 27, 33, 227; Ivers, *British Drums on the Southern Frontier,* 155–62, 165–99.

24. In a footnote to "Jekyl-Creek," in *A Relation,* Kimber writes, "*Jekyl-Island,* from whence this Creek derives its Name, is opposite to the South End of St. *Simon's,* and makes with it the Entrance from Sea into St. *Simon's* Sound. . . . A few Rangers are at present settled on *Jekyl.* It is about nine Miles long, and three Miles and an half broad (7)." The island was named by Oglethorpe in 1734 in honor of Sir Joseph Jekyl, a lawyer and statesman who helped support the founding of Georgia; John H. Goff, *Placenames of Georgia,* eds. Francis Lee Utley and Marion R. Hemperley (Athens: University of Georgia Press, 1975), 161.

25. Captain James Gascoigne had served as a lieutenant in South Carolina from 1728 to 1734. He arrived in Georgia from England during the spring of 1736, commanding H. M. Sloop-of-War, *Hawk.* The trustees granted him a five-hundred-acre plot on St. Simons Island, which became known as Gascoigne Bluff; Coleman, ed., *Entry Books,* 187; Ivers, *British Drums on the Southern Frontier,* 61–62. There, as Cate explains, Gascoigne "maintained headquarters for the vessels of Georgia's first Navy. He had a storehouse for supplies, as well as a careening ground for repair of the ships. He was granted five hundred acres for his plantation and built a substantial house and several outhouses." In 1739 Gascoigne sold the plantation and returned to England; E. Merton Coulter, and Albert B. Saye, eds., *A List of the Early Settlers of Georgia* (Athens: University of Georgia Press, 1949), 75. During the invasion of 1742 the Spanish landed at and took possession of Gascoigne Bluff; *Early Days of Coastal Georgia,* 226.

26. The notion that animals deteriorated in the New World would be most fully developed by Georges Louis Leclerc, Comte de Buffon during the second half of the eighteenth century. Kimber's reference to the superior size of European horses shows that the idea was already well established before Buffon. For the most thorough treatment of the subject, *see* Antonello Gerbi, *The Dispute of the New World: The History of a Polemic, 1750–1900,* trans. Jeremy Moyle (Pittsburgh: University of Pittsburgh Press, 1973).

27. Call'd *Sounds,* as, in this Rout, *Sapola, Ossabaw, St. Catherine's, Ogechee,* &c. taking their Names from those Islands. These are all good Har-

bours, but, with little Wind, very dangerous Navigation for open Boats. (*Kimber's note*)

28. As the Live Oak, Water Oak, Swamp Oak, Marsh Oak, Holy Oak, &c. Live Oak is much more hard and solid than the Wood of *Brazil*, and full as heavy. I believe it would turn to Account to import some Quantity of this Wood for the Use of Refiners, &c. who require very strong Fires. (*Kimber's note*)

29. You'll see, in this Part of the World, Trees dress'd from the Tops to the Roots in this Vegetable, which hangs together Net-wise, and quite obscures the Tree: It seems an excellent Provision of Nature, for the Subsistence of some Orders of Creatures, who, especially in the Winter Season, feed much on it; nor is it unuseful to Man, it has often afforded us comfortable Beds, Pillows, and Tinder. (*Kimber's note*)

30. The Possum is a Creature siz'd like an Hare, and very remarkable for its false Belly, in which, at a Time of Danger, her young Ones creep, and so she carries them off with her; it eats like Pig, and is very nourishing. (*Kimber's note*)

31. The Raccoon is delicate eating, somewhat tasted like Lamb; its Pizzle is very commonly us'd as a Tobacco stopper. Squirrels are also most delicious Food. (*Kimber's note*)

32. Paeans to the mockingbird are commonplace within the literature of the colonial South. In his 1705 *History of Virginia*, Robert Beverley wrote, "the merry Birds too, join their pleasing Notes to this rural Consort, especially the Mock-birds, who love Society so well, that whenever they see Mankind, they will perch upon a Twigg very near them, and sing the sweetest wild Airs in the World: But what is most remarkable in these Melodious Animals, they will frequently fly at small distances before a Traveller, warbling out their Notes several Miles an end, and by their Musick, make a Man forget the Fatigues of his Journey"; *The History and Present State of Virginia*, ed. Louis B. Wright (Chapel Hill: University of North Carolina, 1947), 298. Kimber's immediate source is Richard Lewis's "Journey from Patapsko to Annapolis":

> But what is *He* [The Mock Bird], who perch'd above the rest,
> Pours out such various Musick from his Breast!
> His Breast, whose Plumes a cheerful White display,
> His quiv'ring Wings are dress'd in sober Grey.
> Sure, all the *Muses*, this their Bird inspire!
> And *He*, alone, is equal to the Choir
> Of warbling Songsters who around him play,
> While, Echo like, *He* answers ev'ry Lay.
> The chirping *Lark* now sings with sprightly Note,
> Responsive to her Strain *He* shapes his Throat:
> Now the poor widow'd *Turtle* wails her Mate,
> While in soft Sounds *He* cooes to mourn his Fate.
> Oh, sweet Musician, thou dost far excel
> The soothing Song of pleasing *Philomel!*
>
> (lines 74–86)

Lewis's poem had appeared in Isaac Kimber's *London Magazine* 2 (April 1733): 204–7; J. A. Leo Lemay, *A Calendar of American Poetry in the Colonial Newspapers and Magazines and in the Major English Magazines Through 1765* (Worcester: American Antiquarian Society, 1972), no. 258. As Kimber later admits, he carried a copy of Lewis' poem with him during his travels; see below, 52.

Kimber himself would later use the mockingbird for poetic purposes in "The American Song," a poem that appears in *The History of the Life and Adventures of Mr. Anderson* (1754) at a point where the hero Tommy is lamenting his separation from his lover Fanny Barlow. The following two stanzas from the poem also echo Lewis, both in imagery and diction:

III

More pleasing far the turtle's note,
That plaintive, wails his absent mate;
Or *Philomela's* warbling throat,
Lamenting her unhappy fate:
Delightful pair! ye sooth my woe,
And aid the tears that constant flow!

IV

Ye *Mock* birds cease your numerous song,
Nor mimic chaunt amidst the grove;
Tir'd of your lays, the whole day long,
To sadder sounds the wretched rove:
When night has spread its veil around,
I court the *Bull-frogs* croaking sound.

(77)

In a footnote to the "*Mock* birds," Kimber stated "Birds that imitate the song of all others." In a footnote to "*Bull-frogs*," he wrote, "A frog that haunts the marshes, remarkable for a loud melancholy noise."

33. There is a very extraordinary Bird in this Country, which frequents the Sea Beaches, &c. call'd a Sand-Bird, which almost melts in the Mouth, and is every Way like the celebrated Ortolans, tho' you may kill them by Scores every Evening. Snipes are also vastly plenty and good; and, I think, I have seen Woodcocks. (*Kimber's note*)

34. You perceive here, also, thousands of minute Stars, attracting your Eyes, and floating before you; these are Fire-Flies, which look like so many Glow-worms; they are a very small Insect, with some luminous Qualities or Particles, that I never could well examine; but surprize a Stranger much. (*Kimber's note*)

35. *Paradise Lost*, book 4, lines 598–609:

Now came still Ev'ning on, and Twilight gray
Had in her sober Livery all things clad;
Silence accompanied, for Beast and Bird,
They to thir grassy Couch, these to thir Nests
Were slunk, all but the wakeful Nightingale;
She all night long her amorous descant sung;
Silence was pleas'd: now glow'd the Firmament
With living Sapphires: *Hesperus* that led
The starry Host, rode brightest, till the Moon
Rising in clouded Majesty, at length
Apparent Queen unveil'd her peerless light,
And o'er the dark her Silver Mantle threw.

John Milton: Complete Poems and Major Prose, ed. Merritt Y. Hughes (New York: Macmillan, 1957), 292.

36. By the Bull-Frogs, Lizards, Grasshoppers, Marsh Frogs, &c. &c. &c. (*Kimber's note*)

37. Other wild Beasts there are not that I have seen, except the wild Hog or Boar, who is very dangerous to hunt, whose Tracks you often descry by the Holes he has made with his Tusks after the Ground Nuts and Chincopin Nuts. In some Islands there are also Numbers of wild Horses and Cattle. (*Kimber's note*)

38. Kimber's vehement denouncement of the mosquito shows that he remains essentially an outsider among the American colonists. Mosquitoes had been used since the earliest American literature to show how well the outsider had adapted to the New World. William Bradford, writing in 1624, explained, "They are too delicate and unfit to begin new plantations and colonies, that cannot endure the biting of a mosquito. We would wish such to keep at home till at least they be mosquito-proof"; *Of Plymouth Plantation 1620–1647*, ed. Samuel E. Morison (New York: Modern Library, 1981), 159.

39. *A Dictionary of American English* cites Kimber's *Itinerant Observations* for the earliest known usage of the phrase, "Mosquito net."

40. After the Georgia trustees had obtained parliamentary grant to establish military colonies in Georgia to guard against the Spanish, many Scottish Highlanders were recruited. They arrived in Georgia in early 1736 and, under the leadership of John Mohr McIntosh, established New Iverness, which became known as Darien after the failed Scottish settlement at Panama. For more on the Darien settlement, *see* the articles in the special issue of the *Georgia Historical Quarterly* 20 (1936) celebrating the town's bicentenary; Bessie Mary Lewis, "Darien, a Symbol of Defiance and Achievement," 185–198; G. Arthur Gordon, "The Arrival of the Scotch Highlanders at Darien," 199–209; Alexander R. MacDonnell, "The Settlement of the Scotch Highlanders at Darien," 250–62.

41. In 1733 Oglethorpe agreed to pay Captain James MacPherson £200 for building Fort Argyle on the east bank of the Ogeechee and about 8 ¾ miles north of its junction with Canoochee Creek. However, the impracticality of the chosen spot soon became apparent. Work was halted and Oglethorpe ordered MacPherson and his men to move downstream and erect a new fort at a better location. They moved five miles down the west bank of the Ogeechee to a point where the channel widens and a ten-foot bluff rises from the bank of the river. For a thorough discussion and a conjectural illustration of Fort Argyle, *see* Ivers, *British Drums on the Southern Frontier*, 17–22.

42. They often patrole also 300 Miles back in the Country, as far as Mount *Venture*, known by the unfortunate Story of the Murder of *Francis's* Family by the *Yamasee* Indians. (*Kimber's note*) In October 1742 William Francis had been made lieutenant of the troop of English rangers stationed at Mount Venture near the Altamaha River. In early November he traveled to Frederica with fourteen of his men, leaving only four rangers behind to guard the fort and his wife and child. On 7 November a Yamasee war party attacked. At first, they left Mrs. Francis unharmed, but they later returned and tomahawked her and her baby to death. Ivers, *British Drums on the Southern Frontier*, 174–75.

43. The Turkies and Geese are more delicate than those in *Europe;* and, which is almost incredible, I have seen them in all Parts of *North America*, weighing from 40 to 60 Pounds. (*Kimber's note*) As J. A. Leo Lemay has noticed, "The forty-pound wild turkey was a commonplace of seventeenth

and eighteenth-century promotion tracts; indeed, only the more restrained writers specified forty pounds, and frequently the colonial authors said that the wild turkeys reached fifty pounds or more"; "The Text, Tradition, and Themes of 'The Big Bear of Arkansas,'" *American Literature* 47 (1975): 325–26.

44. A 1735 treaty established the boundaries between Creek land and the land granted to the Georgia Trustees. While the treaty granted much of the coastline to the Europeans, the islands of Ossebaw, Sapelo, and St. Catherines were reserved for the Creeks. Oglethorpe renewed the treaty during the summer of 1739. David H. Corkran, *The Creek Frontier 1540–1783* (Norman: University of Oklahoma Press, 1967), 91, 101; Louis DeVorsey, Jr., "Indian Boundaries in Colonial Georgia," *Georgia Historical Quarterly* 54 (1970): 65.

45. Tho' there is no want of Herbs for the Pot in any Wood you pass, particularly wild Spinage, or, as we call it, *Poke*, which is also agreeably medicinal to the Body. (*Kimber's note*)

46. Bears had long been known for their tastiness. William Wood called bear meat a wholesome food source, "esteemed of all men above venison"; *New England's Prospect*, ed. Alden T. Vaughan (Amherst: University of Massachusetts Press, 1977), 43; Thomas Morton also described the taste of bear as good: "His Flesh is esteemed venison, and of a better taste then [*sic*] beefe"; *New English Canaan*, ed. Charles Francis Adams (1883; New York: Burt Franklin, 1967), 210. In the *Secret History of the Line*, William Byrd wrote, "Our men kill'd a Bear of 2 Years Old which was very fat. The Flesh of it hath a good relish, very savory, & inclining nearest to that of Pork. The Fat of this Creature is the least apt to rise in the Stomach of any other. The Men for the most part chose it rather than Venison; the greatest inconvenience was that they eat more Bread with it. We who were not accustom'd to eat this rich Dyet tasted it at first with some squeamishness, but soon came to like it. Particularly our Chaplain lov'd it so passionately, that he wou'd growl like a Wild-Cat over a Squirrel"; *Wiliam Byrd's Histories of the Dividing Line betwixt Virginia and North Carolina*, ed. William K. Boyd (1929; reprint, New York: Dover, 1967), 197.

47. Noble Jones, who came to Georgia on board the *Ann* in 1733 as a carpenter, had, in ten years, become one of colonial Georgia's most prominent citizens. Jones, his family, and their fine home, Wormsloe, have received much scholarly attention. *See* E. Merton Coulter, *Wormsloe: Two Centuries of a Georgia Family* (Athens: University of Georgia Press, 1955); Sarah B. Gober Temple and Kenneth Coleman, *Georgia Journeys: Being an Account of the Lives of Georgia's Original Settlers and Many Other Early Settlers from the Founding of the Colony in 1732 until the Institution of Royal Government in 1754* (Athens: University of Georgia Press, 1961), 268–91; and William M. Kelso, *Captain Jones's Wormslow: A Historical, Archaeological, and Architectural Study of an Eighteenth-Century Plantation Site near Savannah, Georgia* (Athens: University of Georgia Press, 1979).

48. William M. Kelso explains that Kimber's description "mentions or implies several important facts about Wormsloe: (1) it was an 'extraordinary' plantation compared with the several 'pretty Plantations' along the way from St. Catherines; (2) the house was fortified being 'tolerable defensible with small arms'; (3) huts for the marines existed near the house; (4) there was a clearing through the woods from the house to Bethesda; (5) there was a manchecolas (blockhouse type) fort nearby on the water"; *Captain Jones's Wormslow*, 7. On February 19, 1741, Thomas Causton wrote the Trust-

ees that Noble Jones had erected, "what very Justly (when finished) may be called a good house with Convenient Out-Houses for Servants, Cattle, &c he has also fenced and brought into tillage about 14 Acres of Land, he appears very industrious, the Land is of the best kind, and has produced very well" (quoted in Coulter, *Wormsloe*, 25).

49. *Paradise Regained*, book 4, lines 416–18: "sturdiest Oaks / Bow'd thir Stiff necks, loaden with stormy blasts, / Or torn up sheer." Hughes, ed., *John Milton: Complete Poems and Major Prose*, 525.

50. In a letter to Thomas Prince, 25 May 1748, Samuel Fayrweather provides further detail: "The Orphan House . . . is 60 by 40 being three Story High, Its foundation is Brick, 5 feet below the Earth, & the same above, Cellars all through the House.
The first Story, is 10 feet being pannelld Work, Its Second Story is eight feet, being wheather boarded, it has a hip Roof With Dormant Windows. It has a Piazza all around of 10 feet Broad, Near 20 feet high"; Lilla Mills Hawes, ed., "A Description of Whitefield's Bethesda: Samuel Fayrweather to Thomas Prince and Thomas Foxcroft," *Georgia Historical Quarterly* 45 (1961): 364–65.

51. Fayrweather concurs: "There is a beautiful Garden and a fine Orchard containing allmost all Sorts of fruits, Trees, & Herbs which the country will afford"; Hawes, "A Description," 364.

52. Call'd so, tho' some Ways it is only bounded by a Marsh, which is sometimes dry. (*Kimber's note*)

53. Jonathan Barber oversaw the spiritual needs of the orphans at Bethesda. In his journal entry for 22 November 1741, William Stephens described a time Barber came to Savannah to preach: "Mr. Barber from the Orphan House came again and preached upon those end less Topicks of a New Birth, Election, Justification, Sanctification, &c; bringing his hearers into such a Wood, as neither they, nor he himself (I thought) knew the way out of, without another Guide"; *Journal of William Stephens*, 1:11. Despite Stephens' disapproval of Barber's "New Light" doctrine, Barber often visited Savannah on Sundays to preach and developed a small following there.

54. James Habersham (1712–1775) had come to Georgia with Whitefield and had helped establish the Orphan House. He served as both its schoolmaster and its business manager. Before the end of the colonial period, Habersham would become one of the colony's most influential leaders. *DAB*; William Bacon Stevens, "A Sketch of the Life of James Habersham, President of His Majesty's Council in the Province of Georgia," *Georgia Historical Quarterly* 3 (1919): 151–68.

55. For further information on Whitefield's Orphan-House, *see* Thomas P. Haviland, "Of Franklin, Whitefield, and the Orphans," *Georgia Historical Quarterly* 29 (1945): 211–16; Clyde E. Buckingham, "Early American Orphanages: Ebenezer and Bethesda," *Social Forces* 26 (1948): 311–21; and Neil J. O'Connell, "George Whitefield and Bethesda Orphan-House," *Georgia Historical Quarterly* 54 (1970): 41–62.

56. In his journal entry for 31 May 1742, William Stephens provides a good description of the courthouse: "The Court house, which also was the place of publick Worship, receiving Damage from the Rains whenever they fell heavy, which unless cured, must in a little time bring on a decay . . . Wherefore we ventured to lose no time, in getting it repaired as soon as possible. The Body of the house is one entire Building, formed in the inside

Commodiously, with Benches of different Sorts; but only *one* distinguished from the Rest in Degree, beneath which stands a table; both of equal use, for Sacred purposes, or Civil. This was built in the year 1736, and soon after there was added to it a Cloister or Colonade, encompassing the front and both ends of the house, which was not only Ornamental, but very, usefull likewise, in breaking off the violence of the Weather; more Especially the heats, which otherwise did beat so strong upon the house (being all built of Timber) that when a Number of people were in it, 'twas hardly to be born. This Portico so added, had only a flat Roof, which joyned the other a little above the Eaves; but after so long time, wherein frequent experiment has been made finding nothing sufficient to keep out the Rains, But apparent danger of the whole going to Ruin, Upon due Consultation with Skilfull Workmen, it was thought most advisable to make a new Roof for the Whole, wide enough to span it all, even to the extent of the Colonade, and enclosing the Roof of the House"; *Journal of William Stephens*, 1 : 87.

57. There have been many different theories about the origins of Savannah's town plan. For the most recent and most convincing, *see* John W. Reps, "C² + L² + S²?: Another Look at the Origins of Savannah's Town Plan," *Forty Years of Diversity: Essays on Colonial Georgia*, eds. Harvey H. Jackson and Phinzy Spalding (Athens: University of Georgia Press, 1984), 101–51. For references to earlier theories, *see* Reps's documentation.

58. Kenneth Coleman explains that the Trustees' Garden was established at Savannah in 1734 on ten acres east of the settled area: "Here half-acre squares, separated by walks bordered with orange trees, contained different plants. Besides the mulberry trees which were so important in the early days, there were the varieties listed above, and more prosaic fruits, vegetables, and grains. Joseph Fitzwalter, the gardener, favored a practical garden with foodstuffs rather than exotic plants. . . . By 1741 the site contained only a few olive, orange, apple, plum, peach, cherry, mulberry, and locust trees"; *Colonial Georgia: A History* (New York: Charles Scribner's Sons, 1976), 112–13. For the most detailed treatment of the Trustees' Garden, *see* Temple and Coleman, *Georgia Journeys*, 115–44.

59. By the late 1730s several of the Georgia colonists had begun to bristle at Oglethorpe's policies. Specifically, they wanted the opportunity to own slaves and import rum. Slavery, Oglethorpe vehemently argued, would undermine the philanthropic ideals on which the colony was founded. Oglethorpe's opponents, who became known as the malcontents, expressed their views in *A True and Historical Narrative of the Colony of Georgia* (1741), a satirical pamphlet that prompted a flurry of responses and counter-responses. The various pamphlets relating to the controversy are conveniently reprinted in Trevor R. Reese, ed., *The Clamorous Malcontents: Criticisms & Defenses of the Colony of Georgia, 1741–1743* (Savannah: Beehive Press, 1973).

60. William Stephens (1671–1753) came to Georgia in 1737 as secretary to the trustees. After a reorganization of the Georgia government in 1741, he became president of the colony. His home, known as Bewlie (a corruption of Beaulieu) was located on a five-hundred-acre tract at the mouth of the Vernon River, about thirteen miles south of Savannah. *Journal of William Stephens*, passim.

61. Thomas Causton (d. 1746), who had come to Georgia among the earliest colonists on board the *Ann* in 1733, remained one of the most powerful

and contentious of the earliest Georgia colonists. He served as keeper of the Trustees store and rose from Savannah's third bailiff to its first bailiff by the end of 1734. *See* Temple and Coleman, *Georgia Journeys.*

62. Harold E. Davis explains: "Savannah was endowed by nature to be an important port. At Tybee, where the river entered the ocean, there was fifteen feet of water at low tide and twenty-two at high. Ships of four hundred tons could cross the bar and enter smooth water. There was enough protected water to shelter four hundred vessels at once. One of Oglethorpe's first and most useful projects was the lighthouse at Tybee, a ninety-foot structure of the best pine, set upon cedar piles with brick work about the bottom. The light was a beacon for ships at sea as well as a marker for people of the surrounding lowlands. At one point Oglethorpe inspected the construction and, angered by unsatisfactory progress, imprisoned the man in charge and threatened to hang him. Tybee Light, thus sped to completion, saved many vessels, but like most public structures of the pre-Revolutionary era, it was always on the verge of collapse. The first lighthouse blew down in a storm. Its replacement, built in 1741 and 1742, was likewise in danger of falling into the water"; *The Fledgling Province: Social and Cultural Life in Colonial Georgia 1733–1776* (Chapel Hill: University of North Carolina Press, 1976), 52. *See also* Temple and Coleman, *Georgia Journeys, 47–49.*

63. Ivers explains that Fort Prince Frederick, built during the period from 1731 to 1734 as a replacement for Beaufort Fort, "was a small fort one hundred twenty-five by seventy-five feet with tabby walls about five feet thick and four feet high on three sides. One bastion was built on the southwest side. Along the eastern wall was a battery of cannons commanding Port Royal River. A moat with a palisade planted in the bottom may have surrounded the land side, and earth may have been packed against the outside of the tabby wall. Barracks crowded the inside along with a magazine. The garrison varied from two provincials to one hundred British regulars. The Independent Company of Foot, a unit of British regulars, garrisoned the fort until they were transferred to Georgia in 1736. During the next two years provincial soldiers were stationed there. British soldiers from the 42nd Regiment in Georgia provided a garrison from 1738 until about 1744"; *Colonial Forts of South Carolina 1670–1775* (Columbia: University of South Carolina Press, 1970), 67.

64. On 27 June 1743 William Stephens recorded, "At the same time [before noon] Ensign Donn from Frederica Stopping here in his way to Port Royal, proceed[ed] on his passage thither, in order to relieve a Subaltern Officer who was on Duty with some men at Fredericks Fort"; *Journal of William Stephens*, 1:220.

65. The town of Beaufort, named after Henry, Duke of Beaufort, a lord proprietor, had been laid out before 16 February 1716. Development had been sluggish, so in 1740 an act was passed to encourage development. The act stipulated that every person granted a lot in Beaufort was required within three years to erect a "tenantable house of at least thirty feet in length and fifteen feet in breadth and with at least one brick chimney"; Henry A. M. Smith, "Beaufort—The Original Plan and the Earliest Settlers," *South Carolina Historical and Genealogical Magazine* 9 (1908): 143, 147. Kimber's brief remark suggest that the new act was working.

66. See our *Mag.* for *Aug.* 1745, p. 395. (*Kimber's note*) *See* above, 26.

67. See our *Mag.* for *Decem.* 1745, p. 604. (*Kimber's note*).

68. See the two Pieces sign'd *Americus;* one in our *Mag.* for *September,* 1744, p. 444–46; the other in our *Mag.* for *November* the same year, p. 541–46. (*Kimber's note*)

69. The Ports of *America* are filled with various Kinds of Vessels, not over common in very long voyages in *Europe;* where three Mast Vessels are generally used, as much on account of their better Accommodations for living, as on account of the more tempestuous Seas they trade in; for most commonly the Coasts of *America* and the *West Indies* are a very safe and pleasant Navigation, and long Voyages have been made in very small Craft. Sloops and Schooners are the general Built they run upon, and they are very adroit in the Contrivance of them, particularly at *Bermudas,* where they build prodigious Numbers for Sale. They have also Galleys, Settees, Perriaguas, Launches, &c. too many to mention. I can't imagine the experienced Sailor would ever choose to trust himself in any Thing preferably to a three Mast vessell; for as to Sloops, for Instance, 'tis plain you have but one Dependence, and may be swallowed up before you can remedy your Loss. (*Kimber's note*)

70. The name of this tiny island is also spelled "Nutten and "Nutting." It is now known as Governors Island. Dr. Alexander Hamilton, visiting the island shortly after Kimber, provides the best contemporary description: "Having a contrary wind and an ebb tide, we dropt anchor about half a mile below New York and went ashore upon Nutting Island, which is about half a mile in dimension every way, containing about 60 or 70 square acres. We there took in a cask of spring water. One half of this island was made into hay, and upon the other half stood a crop of good barley, much dammaged by a worm which they have here which, so soon as their barley begins to ripen, cuts off the heads of it. There lived an old Scots-Irishman upon this island with his family in a ruinous house, a tennant of the Governour's to whom the island belongs durante officio. This old man treated us with a mug of ship beer and entertained us with a history of some of the adventures of the late Governour Cosby upon that island. It is called Nutting Island from its bearing nuts in plenty, but what kind of nuts they are I know not, for I saw none there. I saw myrtle berrys growing plentifully upon it, a good deal of juniper, and some few plants of the ipecacuan. The banks of the island are stonny and steep in some places. It is a good place to erect a battery upon to prevent an enimy's approach to the town, but there is no such thing, and I believe that an enimy might land on the back of this island out of reach of the town battery and plant cannon against the city or even throw boombs from behind the island upon it"; *Gentleman's Progress: The Itinerarium of Dr. Alexander Hamilton, 1744,* ed. Carl Bridenbaugh (Chapel Hill: University of North Carolina Press, 1948), 50.

71. Sandy Hook juts five miles into the sea from the New Jersey coast. A lighthouse was not erected there until 1763. *New Jersey: A Guide to Its Present and Past* (1939; St. Clair Shores, Michigan: Somerset, 1973), 678.

72. Worm Fences. (*Kimber's note*) *Dictionary of American English:* "A fence built with rails laid so that the ends cross each other at angles; a zigzag rail fence."

73. Originally called Barendegat, Dutch for breaker's inlet. *New Jersey: A Guide to Its Present and Past,* 559.

74. Originally named Cape Cornelius in 1620 by Captain Cornelius May of the Dutch West India Company, the cape was also known as Cape James

after 1629. Before the end of the seventeenth century, however, the Dutch name "Hinlopen" which had been given to the nearby "False Cape" (Fenwick's Island) was applied to the cape itself. A lighthouse had been erected there in 1725. *Delaware: A Guide to the First State* (1938; St. Clair Shores, Michigan: Somerset, 1973), 497, 498.

75. I forget where my Memory furnish'd me with these Lines. (*Kimber's note*)

76. These are large flat-bottom'd Boats, capable of carrying some Tons of Goods, and used in the Tobacco Countries to unlade Vessels with. They have also a Kind of Sloop, clumsily built, which may be called *Tobacco Druggers*, of 70 or 80 Tons Burden. (*Kimber's note*)

77. Kimber would later set his novel, *The History of the Life and Adventures of Mr. Anderson* (1754), at Senepuxon.

78. See Letter from a Son in a distant Part of the World, March 2, 1743, in *London Magazine*, July, 1744, p. 355. (*Kimber's note*) "A Letter from a Son," lines 143–50; *see* 85.

79. Robert Beverley suggests that "some *Vertuosi* make an agreeable kind of Beer" from persimmons; *The History and Present State of Virginia*, 130. Robert Bolling's 1763 hudibrastic poem "Neanthe," suggests that persimmon beer was an economical drink. Describing the title character's parents, Bolling writes,

> By Dint of rigid Industry,
> Still more by close Economy—
> (Their Drink Persimon Beer, their Food
> Crabs, Oysters by the Bay bestowd)
> They scraped together an Estate,
> That gave them with their Neighbours Weight

See J. A. Leo Lemay, "Southern Colonial Grotesque: Robert Bolling's 'Neanthe,'" *Mississippi Quarterly* 35 (1982): 114.

80. The site that became Snow Hill was originally part of a tract patented by Colonel William Stevens in 1676. It was named after a London suburb of the time. Two year later, Stevens sold it to Henry Bishop. The Maryland Assembly's 1683 Act for the Advancement of Trade stipulated that five towns be founded in Somerset County. In 1686 the Snow Hill tract was chosen as the site of a trade-and-export town on the Pocomoke River. In 1742, when Worcester County was established, Snow Hill became the county seat. *Maryland: A Guide to the Old Line State* (1940; St. Clair Shores, Michigan: Somerset Publishers, 1973), 443.

81. The issue of clerical salaries had been a heated one for some time. For the most delightful contemporary treatment, *see* Thomas Cradock, "The Maryland Divine," *The Poetic Writings of Thomas Cradock, 1718–1770*, ed. David Curtis Skaggs (Newark: University of Delaware Press, 1983), 166–69.

82. Made of *Indian* Corn, or Rice, pounded. (*Kimber's note*)

83. *Indian* Meal, pounded or ground with the Husks, and fry'd. *Great Homine* has Meat or Fowl in it. (*Kimber's note*) In *The History of the Tuesday Club*, Dr. Alexander Hamilton's persona, Loquacious Scribble exclaims, "Homony, I affirm, to be a good wholesome and Simple Dish, very well adapted for nourishment, and The more Simple our food is, the more kindly and agreeable it is to our Stomachs"; *The History of the Ancient and Honorable*

Tuesday Club, ed. Robert Micklus (Chapel Hill: University of North Carolina Press, 1990), 2:207.

84. The Shell of a Fruit so called. Some of them hold two Quarts. (*Kimber's note*)

85. What is said here is most strictly true, for their Manner of Living is quite generous and open: Strangers are sought after with Greediness, as they pass the Country, to be invited. Their Breakfast Tables have generally the cold Remains of the former Day, hash'd or fricasseed; Coffee, Tea, Chocolate, Venison-Pasty, Punch, and Beer, or Cyder, upon one Board: Their Dinner, good Beef, Veal, Mutton, Venison, Turkies and Geese, wild and tame, Fowls boil'd and roasted; and perhaps somewhat more, as Pies, Puddings, &c. for Desert: Suppers the same, with some small Addition, and a good hearty Cup to precede a Bed of Down: And this is the constant Life they lead, and to this Fare every Comer is welcome. (*Kimber's note*)

86. "Cymon and Iphigenia," lines 400–4, 407–8. Kimber omitted the two intervening lines (lines 405–6): "This was the morn when, issuing on the guard, / Drawn up in rank and file they stood prepared." *John Dryden*, ed. Keith Walker (New York: Oxford University Press, 1987), 848.

87. Former Governor Alexander Spotswood had originally been chosen to command a group of four hundred Virginia soldiers to assist the British forces in their attack of Cartagena on the northern coast of South America. After Spotswood's unexpected death, Governor William Gooch assumed the command. The attack, led by Vice-Admiral Vernon, proved a dismal failure. *DAB*; Pares, *War and Trade in the West Indies*, 91–93.

88. A Negro Quarter, is a Number of Huts or Hovels, built at some Distance from the Mansion-House; where the Negroes reside with their Wives and Families, and cultivate, at vacant Times, the little Spots allow'd them. They are, indeed, true Pictures of Slavery, which begets Indolence and Nastiness. (*Kimber's note*) In *The History of the Life and Adventures of Mr. Anderson* (1754), Kimber would further describe the spatial relation between the Negro quarters and the plantation home. At one point Barlow, the plantation owner, left his house to visit the Negro quarter. Kimber wrote: "*Barlow* was out of hearing; for the minute he left the room, he walked down to the *Negro* quarter near his house, and so was half a mile distant by this time" (50). For good treatments of Virginia and Maryland slave housing, *see* Dell Upton, "White and Black Landscapes in Eighteenth-Century Virginia," *Places: A Quarterly Journal of Environmental Design* 2, no. 2 (1985): 59–72; George W. McDaniel, *Heart and Home: Preserving a People's Culture* (Philadelphia: Temple University Press, 1982).

89. A Negro just purchased from the *Guinea-man*. 'Tis really shocking to be present at a Mart of this Sort; where the Buyers handle them as the Butchers do Beasts in *Smithfield*, to see if they are Proof in Cod, Flank, and Shoulders. And the Women, who have Plantations, I have seen mighty busy in examining the Limbs, Size, and Abilities of their intended Purchases. I do not speak this of *Maryland*; for I never saw a Lady at the Market there, but have elsewhere in *America*. (*Kimber's note*)

90. For a further explanation of this comment, *see* Allan Kulikoff, "The Origins of Afro-American Society in Tidewater Maryland and Virginia, 1700 to 1790," *William and Mary Quarterly*, 3d ser., 35 (1978): 236.

91. Kimber further developed these ideas in *The History of the Life and Adventures of Mr. Anderson* (1754). When Tom the protagonist starts getting

too close to Fanny Barlow, her father banishes him to a distant part of his plantation and makes him an overseer. Tom soon has the plantation in fine working order: "By his sweet treatment of the *Negroes*, he gained their good-will, and shewed that kindness and clemency to those miserable creatures will make them more serviceable than cruelty and brutality; for, in the first fortnight, he had more tobacco hoed and housed, and more work of every sort completed, than was ever seen upon that plantation before" (73–74).

92. William Bull Sr. (1683–1755), a close friend of James Oglethorpe, had become lieutenant governor of South Carolina in 1738 and served until 1743. In 1739 he was actively involved in quelling a slave rebellion, an event which led to reform in the slave laws of South Carolina. In 1740, under Bull's administration, a new slave code was established that was designed to mini-mize cruelty to the slaves. *DAB;* M. Eugene Sirmans, *Colonial South Carolina: A Political History, 1663–1763* (Chapel Hill: University of North Carolina Press, 1966), 208–9.

93. A Cowskin is so called, from being a large Thong from the Hide of that Animal, twisted into the Shape of a Swish Horse-Whip, and as hard as a Bull's Pizzle. The common Method is to tie them up by the Hands to the Branch of a Tree, so that their Toes can hardly touch the Ground; but in the *West-Indies*, they are so habituated to ill Usage, and their Spirits so sunk, that the Overseer need only bid them cast up their Arms over their Heads, which the poor Creatures readily do, and then the Torturer taking a Run to him, lashes him; and this Discipline is repeated sometimes forty Times: Hardly a Negro but bears the Marks of Punishment in large Scars on his Back and Sides. (*Kimber's note*) Kimber would later reuse the word *cowskin* several times in *The History of the Life and Adventures of Mr. Anderson* (1754), once parenthetically defining it as "a twisted thong with which they [the Maryland planters] usually discipline their *Negroes.*" Kimber's use of the term antedates the earliest known usage of the term listed in the *Dictionary of American English*, which lists a 1799 article from the Philadelphia *Aurora* that used the term as a verb.

94. Job 3 : 17. Kimber would later quote the same verse in a discussion of indentured servitude in *The History of the Life and Adventures of Mr. Anderson* (1754), 37.

95. *An Essay on Man: Epistle I*, line 108. Pope, *An Essay on Man*, ed. Maynard Mack (London: Methuen, 1950), 28: "Where slaves once more their native land behold, / No fiends torment, no Christian thirst for gold!"

96. Potosi, a town in present-day Bolivia, had long been known for its silver mining since silver ore had been discovered there during the mid-sixteenth century.

97. For more on transported convicts and indentured servants, *see* Abbot Emerson Smith, *Colonists in Bondage: White Servitude and Convict Labor in America, 1607–1776* (Chapel Hill: University of North Carolina Press, 1947); A. Roger Ekirch, *Bound for America: The Transportation of British Convicts to the Colonies, 1718–1775* (New York: Oxford University Press, 1987); Kenneth Morgan, "English and American Attitudes towards Convict Transportation, 1718–1775," *History* 72 (1987): 416–31; Kevin J. Hayes, "The Board of Trade's 'cruel' Sarcasm': A Neglected Franklin Source," *Early American Literature* 28 (1993): 171–76.

98. The anecdote inspired the plot of Kimber's later novel, *The History of the Life and Adventures of Mr. Anderson* (1754). See W. Gordon Milne, "A

Glimpse of Colonial America As Seen in an English Novel of 1754," *Maryland Historical Magazine* 42 (1987): 239–52.

99. A *Branch* is a Stream running across the Road, from some neighbouring Creek or River. (*Kimber's note*)

100. Or Tavern, Eating-house, or Inn. (*Kimber's note*)

101. In 1745 William Logan described Snow-Hill as a "poor Miserable little town"; "William Logan's Journal," 3.

102. And live most prodigiously hard. At Night, you need only tether them out, and they pick Subsistence enough in their Station: I have known them go six Days Journey without a Feed of Corn; having nothing but the Stalks of *Indian* Wheat, and such other Litter as they could pick up. (*Kimber's note*)

103. William Logan described the road from Snow-Hill in detail: "there are no publick Houses so that Travellers are obliged to impose on Gentlemen, a practice I cannot yet come into. Bated in the Woods ab^t one o'clock & eat some Bisket & Cheese but could get no good Water any where on the Road; the Publick Road running within a Mile & less of the Sea-Side so that the water is Brackish.

"There are Trees Marked or Posts sett up with the Distance to any publick Place Every Mile which is convenient to Travellers as the Road is very lonesome, the People's Houses being Out of sight from the Road"; "William Logan's Journal," 3.

104.

> Their bursting buds the tender leaves disclose;
> The tender leaves in downy robes appear,
> Trembling, they seem to move with cautious fear,
> Yet now to life, and strangers to the air.

We suppose the Author suppress'd these Lines, in the same Description, because the Season of the Year was different when he was there. The whole Poem is in our *Magazine* for April 1733, p. 204–207. It was first publish'd in a Paper called the *Weekly Register*, since deceas'd. (*Kimber's note*), above. Richard Lewis, "A Journey from Patapsko to Annapolis," lines 120–34; *An Early American Reader*, ed. J. A. Leo Lemay (Washington, D.C.: United States Information Agency, 1988), 562–63.

105. Letter to A Son, sign'd Sophronius, in your Mag. for July 1744, P. 343. ANONYMOUS. (*Kimber's note*).

106. While Euclid's *Elements of Geometry* may seem an unusual book to take traveling, it is important to understand that the conduct books of the period generally recommended that travelers describe prominent buildings and military fortifications during the course of their travels. Kimber may have lacked confidence in his geometrical abilities and thus carried along Euclid to help him understand and describe the architecture he encountered.

107. Sirmans suggests that by the early 1740s South Carolina's longstanding paper money problem had been solved; *Colonial South Carolina*, 205–6, 221. Kimber's remarks, which Sirmans does not cite, suggest that the problem was far from over.

108. In *The Life and Adventures of Joe Thompson* (1750; reprint, New York: Garland, 1974), 2:81, Kimber cited a letter from his protagonist's friend, William Failer, in which Failer explains, "There are some other Things essential to the Affairs of *America* that I wish could be laid before you, such as the Nature and Use of a Paper Currency there, the Necessity of putting it

under a proper Regulation, and the unavoidable Consequence of utterly ruining our Trade in, and with these Colonies, should it be totally prohibited."

For specific information on Georgia's currency problems, *see* William Estill Heath, "The Early Colonial Money System of Georgia," *Georgia Historical Quarterly* 19 (1935): 145–60. For a general overview of currency issues throughout the colonies, *see* Leslie V. Brock, *The Currency of the American Colonies, 1700–1764: A Study in Colonial Finance and Imperial Relations* (1941; New York: Arno, 1975).

109. Kimber's remarks here anticipate his comment in the preface to *The Ladies Complete Letter-Writer* (London: for the editor, and sold by T. Lownds, 1763): "I have not borrowed from the *French* Letter-Writers; the Manners of their Females are such as would sit but ill upon the *English* Ladies, and there is a flimsy Kind of Gaiety in the Epistolary Correspondence, that would be displeasing to the more grave and sensible Turn of Mind of the *British* Fair" (ii).

110. Kimber would reiterate this notion in the "Editor's Preface" to *The Life and Adventures of Joe Thompson:* "Others [other writers], to excite Mirth, and entertain the Reader's vicious Taste, have represented such strange and ludicrous Characters, as sure never existed, but in Imagination; uncouth as the Characters of the famed *Rabelais*, which no one can liken to any Thing but those shadowy, fantastic Representations of the *baseless Fabric of a Vision*, that sport in our Fancies, when laid in the Arms of Sleep" (1:xii).

111. Kimber would quote the same four lines, still attributed to the "Incert. Auct." on the title page of *The Ladies Complete Letter-Writer.*

112. The Reverend William Dawson (1704–1752) had been the Professor of Moral and Intellectual Philosophy since 1729. Upon the death of James Blair in 1743, Dawson became president of the College of William and Mary; Lyon Gardiner Tyler, *Encyclopedia of Virginia Biography* (New York: Lewis Historical Publishing Company, 1915), 1:156.

113. In *The History of the Life and Adventures of Mr. Anderson* (1754), Kimber would describe Mr. Ferguson, a graduate of the University of Glasgow and formerly an indentured servant to Mr. Barlow, as a person who "at the expiration of his time, had set up for himself in a small neighbouring plantation, where he also practiced the business of a surgeon and schoolmaster, and had lately been talked of by *Barlow* to instruct his daughter in reading and writing" (20).

114. Describing Fanny Barlow, the heroine of *The History of the Life and Adventures of Mr. Anderson* (1754), Kimber would write, "*Fanny*, as to temper, had all her mother, but nothing of her father about her, and, as the plantations lie pretty wide from each other, and the prudence of her mother had kept her from any intercourse with the children of their *Negroes*, she had seen few white children" (14).

115. Here, Kimber echoes Hugh Jones, *The Present State of Virginia*, ed. Richard L. Morton (Chapel Hill: University of North Carolina Press, 1956), 84, who wrote, "They [the Virginians] are such lovers of riding, that almost every ordinary person keeps a horse; and I have known some to spend the morning in ranging several miles in the woods to find and catch their horses only to ride two or three miles to church, to the court-house, or to a horse-race." In *The History of the Life and Adventures of Mr. Anderson* (1754), Kimber would record a conversation in which young Mr. Carter attempts to woo Fanny Barlow. He claims that they will "keep coach, and I'm sure it

will be the first kept in *Worcester* county, 'pon my soul will it—then who but we—ha? what a figure you'll make at church, and I at the *Court-house* . . . I'm quite tir'd of going like the petty planters on horseback." In a footnote to the passage, Kimber wrote, "In *Maryland* and *Virginia* they are such great horseman, that a planter will go or send 5 miles to fetch his horse up, in order to ride one mile to church" (238–39).

116. The Author was again in *Maryland* for some Time, and many of the detach'd Observations were made then, though he chose to interweave them with this short Tour. (*Kimber's note*)

117. "A Letter from a Son," lines 155–62; *see* 85.

118. Virginia's eastern shore has received considerable scholarly treatment. *See* Jennings Cropper Wise, *Ye Kingdome of Accawmacke or the Eastern Shore of Virginia in the Seventeenth Century* (Richmond: Bell Book and Stationery Co., 1911); Susie M. Ames, *Studies of the Virginia Eastern Shore in the Seventeenth Century* (Richmond: Deitz Press, 1940); and Ralph T. Whitelaw, *Virginia's Eastern Shore: A History of Northampton and Accomack Counties* (1951; reprint, Gloucester, Mass.: Peter Smith, 1968).

119. *A Dictionary of American English* cites *Itinerant Observations* as the earliest recorded usage of the word "buckskin." Dr. Alexander Hamilton was also using the word at approximately the same time and the *Dictionary of Americanisms* cites Hamilton's *Itinerarium* as the earliest recorded usage. Hamilton told a fellow traveler who was contemplating a trip through Maryland, "the most dangerous wild beasts in these woods were shaped exactly like men, and they went by the name of buckskins, or bucks, tho they were not bucks neither but something, as it were, betwixt a man and a beast"; *Gentleman's Progress*, 123. Kimber himself would reuse the term in *The Life and Adventures of Joe Thompson*. In chapter 44, Thompson's friend, William Prim, describes meeting a young lady: "You know, *Thompson*, that I have a good Address, and a ready Fluency of Speech; and I put myself forward in every Thing that could be agreeable to my Friend, and these Ladies; insomuch, that *Fanny*, I believe, soon perceived me anotherguess Creature than the *Buckskins*, a Term the Towns-people make use of, jocosely, to distinguish the Country Planters, who had made Love to her" (2 : 128–29). For the best discussion of the term, *see* J. A. Leo Lemay, "The Frontiersman from Lout to Hero: Notes on the Significance of the Comparative Method and the Stage Theory in Early American Literature and Culture," *Proceedings of the American Antiquarian Society* 88 (1978): 190–91.

120. Magothy Bay. In *The History of the Life and Adventures of Mr. Anderson* (1754), Kimber describes his protagonist's return to Maryland after a long absence: "As *Senepuxon* inlet was but shallow, he advis'd the Captain to stand into the great bay of *Chespeak*, and cast anchor close to the *Eastern* shore in *Magidi* bay, which they did accordingly" (213–14).

121. A very small and dangerous sort of *Canoa*, liable to be overturn'd by the least Motion of the Sitters in it. The *Negroes* manage them very dextrously, with a Paddle. (*Kimber's note*) The *Dictionary of American English* cites Kimber's *Itinerant Observations* as the earliest known usage of the word *punt* to apply to these indigenous American watercraft.

122. This Gentleman died afterwards in *Jamaica*. (*Kimber's note*)

123. "A Letter from a Son," lines 128–42; *see* 84–85.

124. See some Lines under the Title of *Fidenia, or the Explanation*, in the

London Magazine, March 1744, page 147. (*Kimber's note*) The poem is reprinted, 75–77.

125. Richard Glover, *Leonidas: A Poem* (Dublin: R. Reilly for J. Smith and W. Bruce, 1737), lines 89–95:

> As o're the western waves, when ev'ry storm
> Is hush'd within its cavern, and a breeze
> Soft-breathing lightly with its wings along
> The slacken'd cordage glides, the sailor's ear
> Perceives no sound throughout the vast expanse;
> None, but the murmurs of the gliding prowe,
> Which slowly parts the smooth and yielding main

Kimber would reuse these same lines in *The Life and Adventures of Joe Thompson*, 2:108.

126. Kimber borrowed his diction from Richard Lewis' "Journey from Patapsko to Annapolis." Richard Beale Davis, *Intellectual Life in the Colonial South, 1585–1763* (Knoxville: University of Tennessee Press, 1978), 3: 1465, 1466.

127. The Carolina parrot, *Conuropsis carolinensis*.

128. Kimber made similar comparisons between the American Indians and the ancient Britons in *A Relation*. At one point he describes them as "the former uncultivated Inhabitants of *Britain*, whom *Tacitus* mentions" (16). Later in *A Relation*, he says if you, "view them without Prejudice, you will perceive some Remains of an ancient Roughness and Simplicity, common to all the first Inhabitants of the Earth; even to our own dear Ancestors, who, I believe, were much upon a Level with these *Indian* hunting Warriors." (17). In both the present work and in *A Relation*, Kimber is applying the comparative method and the stage theory. For the best treatment of these Enlightenment notions as they were applied in early America, *see* Lemay, "The Frontiersman from Lout to Hero."

129. This *Indian* was kill'd at the Head of his People, valiantly fighting, as an Auxiliary Party to the *English*, by the *Yamasees*, in the Year 1743, and was interr'd with military Honours at *Fort William*. He was Son to the Great *Mico Tomo Chachi*, and always bore an extreme Regard to the *English*. He had however this Satisfaction, to see most of the *Yamasees* cut off before he expir'd. (*Kimber's note*). Toonahowi was Tomochichi's nephew and heir. When James Oglethorpe traveled to England in 1734, he brought the two with him, introduced them to King George II and Queen Caroline, had their portrait painted by Cornelis Verelst, and generally showed them off throughout London. After returning to Georgia, Toonahowi and Tomochichi remained loyal to Oglthethorpe. *See* John Pitts Corry, *Indian Affairs in Georgia, 1732–1756* (Philadelphia, 1936), 71, 123; Corkran, *The Creek Frontier*, 82–89; Phinzy Spalding, *Oglethorpe in America* (Chicago: University of Chicago Press, 1977), 14, 81, 83, 86; and Carl Waldman, *Who Was Who in Native American History: Indians and Non-Indians from Early Contacts through 1900* (New York: Facts on File, 1990), 357–58.

130. Psalms 104:24–26.

131. *Lucan's Pharsalia*, trans. Nicholas Rowe (London : J. Tonson, 1718).

132. For near-contemporary illustrations of Yorktown, *see* E. G. Swem, "Views of Yorktown and Gloucester Town, 1755," *Virginia Magazine of History and Biography* 54 (April 1946): 99–105.

133. Over a decade before, William Hugh Grove described Yorktown: "This City ... is indeed a delicat Village. [It] Stands Elivated on a Sandy hill Like Black heath or Richmond Hill and Like that Overlooks a fine river Broader than the Thames at Those places and [it] has Likewise the prospect of a noble Bay." Gregory A. Stiverson and Patrick H. Butler, III, "Virginia in 1732: The Travel Journal of William Hugh Grove," *Virginia Magazine of History and Biography* 85 (January 1977): 21–22.

134. Philip Lightfoot (1689–1748), a leading merchant and member of the Virginia Council, was one of the wealthiest men of his day and owned a large brick mansion surrounded by an elegant garden in Yorktown near the edge of the bluff behind the water battery. The Nelson family had mansions along both sides of the main street near the center of Yorktown, but Kimber probably refers to the home of Thomas Nelson Jr. (1716–1782) who had been appointed secretary of state of Virginia in 1742. His home was situated on the eastern limits of Yorktown, unobstructed by surrounding buildings. *See* Lyon Gardiner Tyler, *Encyclopedia of Virginia Biography*, vol. 1 (New York: Lewis Historical Publishing Company, 1915), 156–57; Edward M. Riley, "Suburban Development of Yorktown, Virginia, During the Colonial Period." *Virginia Magazine of History and Biography* 60 (1952): 534–35.

Chapter 44 of Kimber's *The Life and Adventures of Joe Thompson* relates the story of Thompson's friend, William Prim, told from the first person point of view. Prim meets a Virginia sea captain named Nelson who employs him and ultimately takes him to his Virginia plantation. Prim describes their arrival: "Mr. *Nelson's* Plantation was upon *James River;* so that when he had delivered some Part of his Cargo at *Gloucester,* we ran up, and anchored at his very Door, saluting his Family with all our Guns" (2:127–28).

135. Edward M. Riley states that the Yorktown Courthouse had been built by Robert Ballard and completed a short time before 16 July 1733, the date when the members of the building company inspected the new courthouse; "The Colonial Courthouses of York County, Virginia," *William and Mary Quarterly*, 2d ser., (1942): 402. A document which has surfaced since Riley did his study suggests that the Yorktown courthouse was almost finished nearly a year before. Traveler William Hugh Grove wrote, "they are Just finishing a Court house or Town hall of Brick with a Piazza before it [which is] very handsom and Convenient"; Stiverson and Butler, "Virginia in 1732," 22.

On the basis of archaeological evidence, Riley describes the courthouse in some detail: "it was built in the shape of a "T," the cross of which was fifty-nine feet, ten inches long and the stem was fifty-two feet. The arrangement of the rooms in the building was clearly shown by the interior walls. The courtroom was in the stem of the building with the judge's bench probably at the rear of the room, as in other similar courthouses. The western wing of the building contained two rooms or offices, while the eastern wing had only one. An open "piazza," probably supported by brick arches, stood in the center of the building, between the two wings, and served as an entrance way"; "Colonial Courthouses," 406.

136. Grove notes that "The roads are Extreamly good thro the whole Country which is levell without Hills or Stones." Stiverson and Butler, "Virginia in 1732," 24. *See also* "Colonial Roads and Wheeled Vehicles," *William and Mary College Quarterly*, 1st ser., 8 (1899–1900): 37–42.

137. For good descriptions of Gloucester, Hampton, and Norfolk, *see* John W. Reps, *Tidewater Towns: City Planning in Colonial Virginia and Maryland*

(Williamsburg: Colonial Williamsburg Foundation, 1972). In *The History of the Dividing Line,* William Byrd described Norfolk: "The Town is built on a level Spot of Ground upon Elizabeth River, the Banks whereof are neither so high as to make the landing of Goods troublesome, or so low as to be in Danger of over-flowing. The Streets are Straight, and adorned with several Good Houses, which Encrease every Day. It is not a Town of Ordinarys and Publick Houses, like most others in this Country, but the Inhabitants consist of Merchants, Ship-Carpenters and other useful Artisans, with Sailors enough to manage their Navigation;" *Wiliam Byrd's Histories,* 36.

138. For further information on the Yorktown battery, *see* Riley, "Suburban Development of Yorktown," 531–32.

139. Frederick Stokes Aldridge explains that Virginia Governor William Gooch "reported in 1742 that the militia comprised 175 companies of foot and 102 troops of horse. The foot companies were of sixty men and the horse, fifty, totaling about 16,000 men, 'above twenty-one years of age and under sixty'"; "Organization and Administration of the Militia System of Colonial Virginia," Ph.D. Diss., American University, 1964, 114.

140. For the best treatment of the buildings at Williamsburg, *see* Marcus Whiffen, *The Public Buildings of Williamsburg, Colonial Capital of Virginia: An Architectural History* (Williamsburg: Colonial Williamsburg, 1958); and Whiffen, *The Eighteenth-Century Houses of Williamsburg: A Study of Architecture and Building in the Colonial Capital of Virginia,* rev. ed., (Williamsburg: Colonial Williamsburg, 1984).

141. Gooch (1681–1751) had became lieutenant governor of Virginia on 8 September 1727 and quickly established a good working relationship with the Virginia colonists as well as with the governing officials in London. *DAB;* Tyler, *Encyclopedia of Virginia Biography,* 1 : 60–61.

142. "A Letter from a Son," lines 59–61, 65–66, 74; *see* below, 83.

143. "A Letter from a Son," lines 80–83; *see* below, 83.

Bibliography

Alden, John, and Dennis C. Landis, eds. *European Americana: A Chronological Guide to Works Printed in Europe Relating to the Americas, 1493–1776*. 5 vols. to date. New York: Readex Books, 1982-.

Aldridge, Frederick Stokes. "Organization and Administration of the Militia System of Colonial Virginia." Ph.D. Diss., American University, 1964.

Allibone, S. Austin. *A Critical Dictionary of English Literature and British and American Authors*. Vol. 2. Philadelphia: J. B. Lippincott, 1870.

Ames, Susie M. *Studies of the Virginia Eastern Shore in the Seventeenth Century*. Richmond: Deitz Press, 1940.

Arthos, John. *The Language of Natural Description in Eighteenth-Century Poetry*. 1949. Reprint, New York: Octagon Books, 1966.

Beverley, Robert. *The History and Present State of Virginia*. Edited by Louis B. Wright. Chapel Hill: University of North Carolina, 1947.

Black, Frank Gees. "Edward Kimber: Anonymous Novelist of the Mid-Eighteenth Century." *Harvard Studies and Notes in Philology and Literature* 17 (1935): 27–42.

Boys, Richard C. "General Oglethorpe and the Muses." *Georgia Historical Quarterly* 31 (1947): 19–29.

Bradford, William. *Of Plymouth Plantation 1620–1647*. Edited by Samuel E. Morison. New York: Modern Library, 1981.

Brock, Leslie V. *The Currency of the American Colonies 1700–1764: A Study in Colonial Finance and Imperial Relations*. 1941. Reprint, New York: Arno, 1975.

Buckingham, Clyde E. "Early American Orphanages: Ebenezer and Bethesda." *Social Forces* 26 (1948): 311–21.

Byrd, William. *William Byrd's Histories of the Dividing Line betwixt Virginia and North Carolina*. Edited by William K. Boyd. 1929. Reprint, New York: Dover, 1967.

Cary, Carson, Norman F. Barka, William M. Kelso, Garry Wheeler Stone, and Dell Upton. "Impermanent Architecture in the Southern American Colonies." *Winterthur Portfolio* 16 (1981).

Cate, Margaret Davis. *Early Days of Coastal Georgia*. St. Simons Island, Ga.: Fort Frederica Association, 1955.

———. "Fort Frederica and the Battle of Bloody Marsh." *Georgia Historical Quarterly* 27 (1943): 111–74.

———. "The Original Houses of Frederica, Georgia: The Hawkins-Davison Houses." *Georgia Historical Quarterly* 40 (1956): 203–12.

———. *Our Yesterdays and Todays: A Story of Brunswick and the Coastal Islands*. Rev. ed. Brunswick, Georgia: Glover Bros., 1930.

Clark, Thomas D. *Travels in the Old South: A Bibliography*. Vol. 1. Norman: University of Oklahoma Press, 1956.

Coleman, Kenneth. *Colonial Georgia: A History*. New York: Charles Scribner's Sons, 1976.

————, ed. *Entry Books of Commissions, Powers, Instructions, Leases, Grants of Land, Etc. by the Trustees*. Vol. 32 of *The Colonial Records of the State of Georgia*. Athens: University of Georgia Press, 1989.

"Colonial Roads and Wheeled Vehicles." *William and Mary College Quarterly*, 1st ser., 8 (1899–1900): 37–42.

Corkran, David H. *The Creek Frontier, 1540–1783*. Norman: University of Oklahoma Press, 1967.

Corry, John Pitts. *Indian Affairs in Georgia, 1732–1756*. Philadelphia, 1936.

Coulter, E. Merton. *Wormsloe: Two Centuries of a Georgia Family*. Athens: University of Georgia Press, 1955.

Coulter, E. Merton, and Albert B. Saye, eds. *A List of the Early Settlers of Georgia*. Athens: University of Georgia Press, 1949.

Cox, Edward, and Edward Berry. *A Catalogue of a Very Large Assortment of . . . Books . . . Which Are to Be Sold by Cox & Berry at Their Store in King-Street, Boston*. [Boston, 1772?].

Davis, Harold E. *The Fledgling Province: Social and Cultural Life in Colonial Georgia, 1733–1776*. Chapel Hill: University of North Carolina Press, 1976.

Davis, Richard Beale. *Intellectual Life in the Colonial South, 1585–1763*. 3 vols. Knoxville: University of Tennessee Press, 1978.

Delaware: A Guide to the First State. 1938. Reprint, St. Clair Shores, Michigan: Somerset, 1973.

DeVorsey, Louis, Jr. "Indian Boundaries in Colonial Georgia." *Georgia Historical Quarterly* 54 (1970): 63–78.

Dictionary of American English on Historical Principles. 4 Vols. Edited by William A. Craigie and James R. Hulbert. Chicago: University of Chicago Press, 1938–1944.

Dictionary of Americanisms on Historical Principles. Edited by Mitford M. Mathews. Chicago: University of Chicago Press, 1951. 2 vols.

Ekirch, A. Roger. *Bound for America: The Transportation of British Convicts to the Colonies, 1718–1775*. New York: Oxford University Press, 1987.

Floyd, M. H., and D. B. Floyd. "Oglethorpe's Home at Frederica." *Georgia Historical Quarterly* 20 (1936): 239–49.

Forster, Antonia. *Index to Book Reviews in England, 1749–1774*. Carbondale and Edwardsville: Southern Illinois University Press, 1990.

Gamble, Thomas. *Savannah Duels and Duellists, 1733–1877*. Savannah: Review Publishing, 1923.

Georgia: A Guide to Its Towns and Countryside. Athens: University of Georgia Press, 1940.

Gerbi, Antonello. *The Dispute of the New World: The History of a Polemic, 1750–1900*. Translated by Jeremy Moyle. Pittsburgh: University of Pittsburgh Press, 1973.

Glover, Richard. *Leonidas: A Poem*. Dublin: R. Reilly for J. Smith and W. Bruce, 1737.

Goff, John H. *Placenames of Georgia.* Edited by Francis Lee Utley and Marion R. Hemperley. Athens: University of Georgia Press, 1975.

Gordon, G. Arthur. "The Arrival of the Scotch Highlanders at Darien." *Georgia Historical Quarterly* 20 (1936): 199–209.

Hamilton, Dr. Alexander. *Gentleman's Progress: The Itinerarium of Dr. Alexander Hamilton 1744.* Edited by Carl Bridenbaugh. Chapel Hill: University of North Carolina Press, 1948.

———. *The History of the Ancient and Honorable Tuesday Club.* Edited by Robert Micklus. 3 vols. Chapel Hill: University of North Carolina Press, 1990.

Haviland, Thomas P. "Of Franklin, Whitefield, and the Orphans," *Georgia Historical Quarterly* 29 (1945): 211–16.

Hawes, Lilla Mills, ed. "A Description of Whitefield's Bethesda: Samuel Fayrweather to Thomas Prince and Thomas Foxcroft." *Georgia Historical Quarterly* 45 (1961): 364–65.

Hayes, Kevin J. "The Board of Trade's '*cruel* Sarcasm': A Neglected Franklin Source." *Early American Literature* 28 (1993): 171–76.

———. *Captain John Smith: A Reference Guide.* Boston: G. K. Hall, 1991.

———. *A Colonial Woman's Bookshelf.* Knoxville: University of Tennessee Press, 1996.

Heath, William Estill. "The Early Colonial Money System of Georgia." *Georgia Historical Quarterly* 19 (1935): 145–60.

Hoffman, Paul P., ed. *Virginia Gazette Daybooks 1750–1752 & 1764–1766.* University of Virginia Library: Microfilm Publications, 1967.

Horace. *Satires, Epistles and Ars Poetica.* Translated by H. Rushton Fairclough. 1929. Loeb Classical Library. Cambridge: Harvard University Press, 1961.

Ivers, Larry E. *British Drums on the Southern Frontier: The Military Colonization of Georgia, 1733–1749.* Chapel Hill: University of North Carolina Press, 1974.

———. *Colonial Forts of South Carolina, 1670–1775.* Columbia: University of South Carolina Press, 1970.

Jones, Charles C. "The English Colonization of Georgia." In *Narrative and Critical History of America.* Edited by Justin Winsor. Vol. 5. Boston: Houghton, Mifflin, 1887.

Jones, George Fenwick. *The Georgia Dutch: From the Rhine and Danube to the Savannah, 1733–1783.* Athens: University of Georgia Press, 1992.

Jones, Hugh. *The Present State of Virginia.* Edited by Richard L. Morton. Chapel Hill: University of North Carolina Press, 1956.

Kelso, William M. *Captain Jones's Wormslow: A Historical, Archaeological, and Architectural Study of an Eighteenth-Century Plantation Site near Savannah, Georgia.* Athens: University of Georgia Press, 1979.

Kennedy, James, W. A. Smith, and A. F. Johnson, *Dictionary of Anonymous and Pseudonymous English Literature (Samuel Halkett and John Laing).* Edinburgh and London: Oliver and Boyd, 1926–1934.

Kimber, Edward. "Eighteenth Century Maryland as Portrayed in the 'Itinerant Observations' of Edward Kimber." *Maryland Historical Magazine* 51 (1956): 315–36.

————. *The General Index to Twenty-Seven Volumes of the London Magazine; viz. from 1732 to 1758 Inclusive.* London: R. Baldwin, 1760.

————. *The History of the Life and Adventures of Mr. Anderson.* 1754. Reprint, New York: Garland, 1975.

————. *The Ladies Complete Letter-Writer.* London: for the editor, and sold by T. Lownds, 1763.

————. *The Life and Adventures of Joe Thompson.* 1750. Reprint, New York: Garland, 1974.

————. "Memoirs of the Life and Writings of the Reverend Mr. Isaac Kimber." In Isaac Kimber, *Sermons on the Most Interesting Religious, Moral, and Practical Subjects.* Edited by Edward Kimber. London: C. and J. Ackers, 1756.

Kimber, Sidney A. "The 'Relation of a Late Expedition to St. Augustine,' with Biographical and Bibliographical Notes on Isaac and Edward Kimber." *PBSA* 28 (1934): 81–96.

————. Introduction to Edward Kimber, *A Relation or Journal of a Late Expedition to the Gates of St. Augustine on Florida.* Boston: Charles E. Goodspeed & Co., 1935.

Kulikoff, Allan. "The Origins of Afro-American Society in Tidewater Maryland and Virginia, 1700 to 1790." *William and Mary Quarterly,* 3d ser., 35 (1978): 236.

Lemay, J. A. Leo. *A Calendar of American Poetry in the Colonial Newspapers and Magazines and in the Major English Magazines Through 1765.* Worcester: American Antiquarian Society, 1972.

————, ed. *An Early American Reader.* Washington, D.C.: United States Information Agency, 1988.

————. "The Frontiersman from Lout to Hero: Notes on the Significance of the Comparative Method and the Stage Theory in Early American Literature and Culture." *Proceedings of the American Antiquarian Society* 88 (1978): 187–223.

————. *Men of Letters in Colonial Maryland.* Knoxville: University of Tennessee Press, 1972.

————. "Southern Colonial Grotesque: Robert Bolling's 'Neanthe.'" *Mississippi Quarterly* 35 (1982): 97–126.

————. *"New England's Annoyances": America's First Folk Song.* Newark: University of Delaware Press, 1985.

————. "The Text, Tradition, and Themes of 'The Big Bear of Arkansas.'" *American Literature* 47 (1975): 321–42.

Lewis, Bessie Mary. "Darien, a Symbol of Defiance and Achievement." *Georgia Historical Quarterly* 20 (1936): 185–98.

Logan, William. "William Logan's Journal of a Journey to Georgia, 1745." *Pennsylvania Magazine of History and Biography* 36 (1912): 1–16, 162–86.

McDaniel, George W. *Heart and Home: Preserving a People's Culture.* Philadelphia: Temple University Press, 1982.

MacDonnell, Alexander R. "The Settlement of the Scotch Highlanders at Darien." *Georgia Historical Quarterly* 20 (1936): 250–62.

MacKall, Leonard L. "The Wymberley Jones De Renne Georgia Library." *Georgia Historical Quarterly* 2 (1918): 63–86.

Manucy, Albert C. *The Fort at Frederica*. Vol. 5 of the Department of Anthropology Notes in Anthropology. Tallahassee: Florida State University, 1962.

Maryland: A Guide to the Old Line State. 1940. Reprint, St. Clair Shores, Mich.: Somerset Publishers, 1973.

Mein, John. *A Catalogue of Mein's Circulating Library*. Boston: [McAlpine and Fleeming,] 1765.

Milne, W. Gordon. "A Glimpse of Colonial America as Seen in an English Novel of 1754." *Maryland Historical Magazine* 42 (1947): 239–52.

Morgan, Kenneth. "English and American Attitudes towards Convict Transportation, 1718–1775." *History* 72 (1987): 416–31.

Morton, Thomas. *New English Canaan*. Edited by Charles Francis Adams. 1883. Reprint, New York: Burt Franklin, 1967.

National Union Catalog: Pre-1956 Imprints. 754 vols. London: Mansell, 1968–1981.

Neal, Willard. "Altamaha." In *Georgia Rivers*, edited by George Hatcher. Athens: University of Georgia Press, 1962: 24–25.

New Jersey: A Guide to Its Present and Past. 1939. Reprint, St. Clair Shores, Michigan: Somerset, 1973.

O'Connell, Neil J. "George Whitefield and Bethesda Orphan-House." *Georgia Historical Quarterly* 54 (1970): 41–62.

Pares, Richard. *War and Trade in the West Indies, 1739–1763*. 1936. Reprint, London: Frank Cass, 1963.

Reese, Trevor R., ed. *The Clamorous Malcontents: Criticisms & Defenses of the Colony of Georgia, 1741–1743*. Savannah: Beehive Press, 1973.

———. *Colonial Georgia: A Study in British Imperial Policy in the Eighteenth Century*. Athens: University of Georgia Press, 1963.

———. *Frederica: Colonial Fort and Town*. St. Simons Island, Ga.: Fort Frederica Association, 1969.

Reps, John W. "$C^2 + L^2 + S^2$?: Another Look at the Origins of Savannah's Town Plan." In *Forty Years of Diversity: Essays on Colonial Georgia*, edited by Harvey H. Jackson and Phinzy Spalding, 101–51. Athens: University of Georgia Press, 1984.

———. *Tidewater Towns: City Planning in Colonial Virginia and Maryland*. Williamsburg: Colonial Williamsburg Foundation, 1972.

Rhodes, Dennis E., and Anna E. C. Simoni, *Dictionary of Anonymous and Pseudonymous English Literature (Samuel Halkett and John Laing): Addenda to Volumes I–VIII*. Edinburgh and London: Oliver and Boyd, 1962.

Riley, Edward M. "The Colonial Courthouses of York County, Virginia." *William and Mary Quarterly*, 2d ser., 22 (1942): 399–414.

———. "The Ordinaries of Colonial Yorktown." *William and Mary Quarterly*, 2d ser., 23 (1943): 8–23.

———. "Suburban Development of Yorktown, Virginia, during the Colonial Period." *Virginia Magazine of History and Biography* 60 (1952): 522–36.

Roscoe, S. John. *John Newberry and His Successors, 1740–1814: A Bibliography*. Wormley, England: Five Owls Press, 1973.

Sirmans, M. Eugene. *Colonial South Carolina: A Political History, 1663–1763*. Chapel Hill: University of North Carolina Press, 1966.

Smith, Abbot Emerson. *Colonists in Bondage: White Servitude and Convict Labor in America, 1607–1776.* Chapel Hill: University of North Carolina Press, 1947.

Smith, Henry A. M. "Beaufort—The Original Plan and the Earliest Settlers." *South Carolina Historical and Genealogical Magazine* 9 (1908): 141–60.

Spalding, Phinzy. *Oglethorpe in America.* Chicago: University of Chicago Press, 1977.

Stephens, William. *The Journal of William Stephens, 1741–1743.* Edited by E. Merton Coulter. Athens: University of Georgia Press, 1958.

Stevens, William Bacon. "A Sketch of the Life of James Habersham, President of His Majesty's Council in the Province of Georgia." *Georgia Historical Quarterly* 3 (1919): 151–68.

Stiverson, Gregory A., and Patrick H. Butler, III. "Virginia in 1732: The Travel Journal of William Hugh Grove." *Virginia Magazine of History and Biography* 85 (1977): 18–44.

Swem, E. G. "Notes and Queries." *Virginia Magazine of History and Biography* 54 (October 1946): 344.

————. "Views of Yorktown and Gloucester Town, 1755." *Virginia Magazine of History and Biography* 54 (1946): 99–105.

Temple, Sarah B. Gober, and Kenneth Coleman. *Georgia Journeys: Being an Account of the Lives of Georgia's Original Settlers and Many Other Early Settlers from the Founding of the Colony in 1732 until the Institution of Royal Government in 1754.* Athens: University of Georgia Press, 1961.

Tepaske, John Jay. "Introduction" to Edward Kimber, *A Relation, or Journal of a Late Expedition.* Gainesville: University Press of Florida, 1976. xi–xliv.

Tyler, Lyon Gardiner. *Encyclopedia of Virginia Biography.* Vol. 1. New York: Lewis Historical Publishing Company, 1915.

Upton, Dell. "White and Black Landscapes in Eighteenth-Century Virginia." *Places: A Quarterly Journal of Environmental Design* 2, no. 2 (1985): 59–72.

Waldman, Carl. *Who Was Who in Native American History: Indians and Non-Indians from Early Contacts through 1900.* New York: Facts on File, 1990.

Watt, Robert. *Bibliotheca Britannica; Or A General Index to British and Foreign Literature.* 4 vols. Edinburgh: for Archibald Constable, 1824.

Whiffen, Marcus. *The Eighteenth-Century Houses of Williamsburg, Va.: A Study of Architecture and Building in the Colonial Capital of Virginia.* Rev. ed. Williamsburg: Colonial Williamsburg, 1984.

————. *The Public Buildings of Williamsburg, Colonial Capital of Virginia: An Architectural History.* Williamsburg, Va.: Colonial Williamsburg, 1958.

Whitelaw, Ralph T. *Virginia's Eastern Shore: A History of Northampton and Accomack Counties.* 1951. Reprint, Gloucester, Mass.: Peter Smith, 1968.

Williams, W. R. "British-American Officers, 1720 to 1763." *South Carolina Historical and Genealogical Magazine* 33 (1932): 183–96; 290–96.

Wise, Jennings Cropper. *Ye Kingdome of Accawmacke or the Eastern Shore of Virginia in the Seventeenth Century.* Richmond: Bell Book and Stationery Co., 1911.

Wood, William. *New England's Prospect.* Edited by Alden T. Vaughan. Amherst: University of Massachusetts Press, 1977.

Yentsch, Anne Elizabeth. *A Chesapeake Family and Their Slaves: A Study in Historical Archaeology.* New York: Cambridge University Press, 1994.

First-Line Index to the Poems

Adieu native plains, where blithsome I've rov'd, ...78

Alas! whilst aching pains declare 92

Foul winds, foul weather vex'd us fore, ...94

From native *Britain's* verdant plains, ...66

Hail, much-lov'd man! forgive the aspiring Muse, ...81

I'll tell you, good sirs, what will make you all smile, ...89

Propitious gale! we hail they healing power! 79

See dusky clouds, the welkin overspread! 68

Soft as the downy plumage of the dove, ...94

Thy charming lines, all pleasing, reach my hands, ...70

What pleasures more rejoice, ...80

Windsor, no more thy chearing views invite. 95

Ye fair, whose worth I so esteem, ...75

Ye gloomy vaults, ye hoary cells, ...96

Index

Accomack County (Virginia), 56–57, 97n. 8
Adams, Charles Francis, 108n. 46
Addison, Joseph, 50; *Cato*, 85, 89
Albany (New York), 17
albacore, 61
Alden, John: *European Americana*, 98n. 19
Aldridge, Frederick Stokes: "Organization and Administration of the Militia System," 121n. 139
Allibone, S. Austin: *Critical Dictionary*, 20, 99n. 34
alligators, 31
Altamaha River, 26, 70, 100n. 1, 107n. 42
American Antiquarian Society: *Proceedings*, 100n. 47, 118n. 119
"Americus" (pseud.). *See* Kimber, Edward
Ames, Susie M.: *Studies of the Virginia Eastern Shore*, 118n. 118
Anglicus, P. V. C. (*pseud.*). *See* Kimber, Edward
Ann (ship), 110n. 61
Annapolis (Maryland), 45, 57
apple, 102n. 8, 110n. 58
Arthos, John: *Language of Natural Description*, 100n. 48
Assateague Inlet, 42
Aurora (Philadelphia), 115n. 93

Bachelor's Redoubt, 28
Ballard, Robert, 120n. 135
Baltimore (Maryland), 57
Barber, Jonathan, 34, 109n. 53
Barendegat (New Jersey), 39, 112n. 73
Barka, Norman F.: "Impermanent Architecture," 100n. 47
bass, 31
bear, 31, 33, 108n. 46

Beaufort (South Carolina), 37, 98n. 13, 111n. 65
Beaufort, Henry, *duke of*, 111n. 65
Bermuda, 112n. 69
Bethesda Orphan House, 33–35, 108n. 48, 109nn. 50–51 and 53–55. *See also* Whitefield, George
Beverley, Robert: *History of Virginia*, 105n. 32, 113n. 78
Bible, 115n. 94, 119n. 130
Bishop, Henry, 113n. 80
Black, Frank Gees, 18; "Edward Kimber," 97n. 12, 98n. 21
Blair, James, 117n. 112
boar, 107n. 37
Bolling, Robert: "Neanthe," 113n. 79
Boltzius, Johann Martin, 103n. 11
Boyd, William K., 108n. 46
Boys, Richard C.: "General Oglethorpe and the Muses," 80
Bradford, William: *Of Plymouth Plantation*, 107n. 38
Bradley (ship), 97n. 9
Bridenbaugh, Carl, 112n. 70
Brindley, James: *History of Inland Navigation*, 19
Brock, Leslie V.: *Currency of the American Colonies*, 117n. 108
Brooke, Frances, 18
Buckingham, Clyde E.: "Early American Orphanages," 109n. 55
Buffon, Georges Louis Leclerc, *comte de*, 104n. 26
Bull, William, Sr., 49, 115n. 92
Butler, Patrick H., III: "Virginia in 1732," 99n. 42, 120nn. 133 and 135–36
Butler, Sámuel, 12
Byrd, William, II: *History of the Dividing Line*, 121n. 137; *Secret History of the Line*, 108n. 46

cassena, 44

Cambridge History of English Literature, 20

Campbell, G. L. (pseud.). *See* Kimber, Edward

Canoochee Creek, 107 n. 40

Cape Charles, 57

Cape Cornelius, 112 n. 74

Cape Fear, 64

Cape Hatteras, 64

Cape Henlopen, 39, 113 n. 74

Cape Henry, 64

Cape James, 112 n. 74

Caroline, Queen, 119 n. 129

Cartagena (Colombia), 47, 114 n. 87

Carteret's Point, 103 n. 12

Cary, Carson: "Impermanent Architecture," 100 n. 47

Cate, Margaret Davis: *Early Days of Coastal Georgia*, 101 n. 2, 102 nn. 7–8 and 10, 103 nn. 13–15, 104 nn. 23 and 25; "Fort Frederica and the Battle of Bloody Marsh," 101 n. 3; "Original Houses," 102 n. 9; *Our Yesterdays and Todays*, 101 n. 1, 102 n. 8

catfish, 31

cattle, 107 n. 37, 109 n. 48

Causton, Thomas, 36, 108 n. 48, 110 n. 61

cedar, 30

Chagres (Panama), 104 n. 22

Charleston (South Carolina), 14, 17, 35, 98 nn. 13–14, 101 n. 5

Chastellux, François Jean, *marquis de*, 24

Chateaubriand, François-René, *vicomte de*, 24

cherry, 110 n. 58

Chesapeake Bay, 13, 23, 77, 97 n. 8, 118 n. 120

China briar, 33

chinquapin, 107 n. 37

Clark, Thomas D.: *Travels in the Old South*, 21, 99 n. 41, 101 n. 3

cockroach, 32

Coleman, Kenneth: *Colonial Georgia*, 103 n. 18, 110 n. 58; *Entry Books*, 102 n. 9, 104 n. 25; *Georgia Journeys*, 108 n. 47, 110 n. 58, 111 nn. 61–62

Collections of the Georgia Historical Society, 20, 99 n. 36

College of William and Mary, 54–55, 63, 117 n. 112

Cooke, William, 79

Corkran, David H.: *Creek Frontier*, 108 n. 44, 119 n. 129

corn, 45–46, 113 nn. 82–83, 116 n. 102

Corry, John Pitts: *Indian Affairs in Georgia*, 119 n. 129

Cosby, William, 112 n. 70

Coulter, E. Merton, 21; *List of the Early Settlers of Georgia*, 104 n. 25; *Wormsloe*, 100 n. 43, 108 n. 47, 109 n. 48

Cowley, Abraham, 12

Cox & Berry (booksellers): *Catalogue*, 98 n. 27

Cradock, Thomas: "Maryland Divine," 113 n. 81; *Poetic Writings*, 113 n. 81

Crebillon, Claude-Prosper, Jolyot de: *Heureux orphelins*, 17–18

Creek Indians, 108 n. 44

Critical Review (London), 20, 99 nn. 29–30

curlew, 32

currency, 45, 52–53, 116 nn. 108–9

Cuthbert (ship), 98 n. 14

cypress, 30

dancing, 56

Darien (Georgia), 32, 95, 97 n. 13

Davis (shipmate of Edward Kimber's), 79

Davis, Harold E.: *Fledgling Province*, 107 n. 41

Davis, Richard Beale, 13; *Intellectual Life in the Colonial South*, 97 n. 7, 100 nn. 46 and 49, 119 n. 126

Dawson, William, 117 n. 112

deer, 31

Delaware, 113 n. 74

Delaware Bay, 57

Delaware River, 39, 57

Demere, Raymond, 27, 102 n. 8

Desbrisay, Albert, 28, 103 n. 13

Devorsey, Louis, Jr., "Indian Boundaries in Colonial Georgia," 108 n. 44

Dickens, Charles, 24

Dictionary of American Biography (DAB), 115 n. 92, 121 n. 141

Dictionary of American English, 21, 101 n. 2, 107 n. 39, 112 n. 72, 115 n. 93, 118 n. 119, 121

Dictionary of Americanisms, 101 n. 2, 118 n. 119

Dictionary of National Biography (DNB), 20, 97 n. 1, 98 n. 23

dolphin, 61

Donegal, Philip, 104 n. 23

Donn, Archibald, 111 n. 64

Driessler, Johann Ulrich, 103 n. 11

Dryden, John, 12, 47; "Cymon and Iphigenia," 114 n. 86

duck, 32

Dunbar, George, 28, 103 n. 15

Ebenezer (Georgia), 102 n. 11

Edinburgh (Scotland), 95

education, 54–55

Ekirch, A. Roger: *Bound for America*, 115 n. 97

Elizabeth River, 121 n. 137

Euclid: *Elements of Geometry*, 52, 116 n. 106

Fairclough, H. Rushton, 89, 103 n. 20

Fenelon, François de Salignac de La Mothe, 87

Fenwick's Island, 113 n. 74

Fielding, Sarah, 18

firefly, 106 n. 34

Floyd, M. H. and D. B.: "Oglethorpe's Home," 102 n. 10

Forster, Antonia: *Index to Book Reviews*, 99 n. 30

Fort Argyle, 32, 107 n. 41

Fort Beaufort, 111 n. 63

Fort Donegal, 104 n. 23

Fort Frederica, 26–27, 100 n. 1, 101 nn. 2 and 5, 102 n. 7, 104 n. 23

Fort Frederick, 36–37, 98 n. 13

Fort Prince Frederick, 111 n. 63

Fort St. Simons, 102 n. 7, 104 n. 23

Fort William, 119 n. 128

Foul Island (Great Britain), 15, 94, 98 n. 14

France, 91

Francis, William, 107 n. 42

Francis, Mrs. William, 107 n. 42

Frederica (Georgia), 13, 14, 16, 22, 26–29, 32, 37, 64–65, 70, 97 n. 13, 100 n. 1, 101 n. 5, 102 n. 9, 107 n. 42, 111 n. 64

Frederica River, 103 n. 14

Frederick Louis, Prince of Wales, 100 n. 1

frog, 107 n. 36

Gamble, Thomas: *Savannah Duels*, 103 n. 13

gardens, 36, 109 n. 51, 110 n. 58

Gascoigne Bluff, 104 n. 25

Gascoigne, James, 29, 104 n. 25

geese, 32, 107 n. 43

George II, King, 100 n. 1, 119 n. 129

Georgia, 11, 16, 22, 26, 37, 64, 97 n. 9, 101 nn. 1–2, 103 n. 18, 104 nn. 23 and 25, 108 n. 47. *See also* references to specific creeks, forts, islands, rivers, and towns

Gerbi, Antonello: *Dispute of the New World*, 104 n. 26

German Village (St. Simons Island), 27, 102 n. 11

Gibraltar, 102 n. 8

Gloucester (Virginia), 57, 62–63, 120 nn. 134 and 137

Glover, Richard, 60; *Leonidas*, 23, 81, 119 n. 125

Goff, John H.: *Placenames of Georgia*, 104 n. 24

Golden Quarter (Maryland), 43, 44, 97 n. 8

Gooch, William, 63–64, 114 n. 87, 121 nn. 139 and 141

Gordon, G. Arthur: "Arrival of the Scotch Highlanders at Daren," 107 n. 40

Governors Island (New York), 38, 112 n. 70

Grant Creek, 103 n. 12

grapevine, 30–31

grasshopper, 107 n. 36

Gravesend (Great Britain), 97 n. 5

Griffiths (ship), 97 n. 5

ground-nut, 107 n. 37

Grove, William Hugh: "Journal," 99 n. 42, 120 nn. 133 and 135–36

Habersham, James, 109 n. 54

Halkett and Laing, 20, 98 n. 35

Hamilton, Dr. Alexander, 112 n. 70;

History of the Tuesday Club, 113 n. 83; *Itinerarium*, 112 n. 70, 118 n. 119

Hampton (Virginia), 63, 120 n. 137

Harrington, Lord, 102 n. 8

Hatcher, George: *Georgia Rivers*, 101 n. 1

Haviland, Thomas P.: "Of Franklin, Whitefield, and the Orphans," 109 n. 55

Hawes, Lilla Mills: "Description of Whitefield's Bethesda," 109 nn. 50–51

Hawk (ship), 104 n. 25

Hawkins, Thomas, 27, 102 n. 9

Hayes, Kevin J.: "Board of Trade's 'cruel Sarcasm,'" 115 n. 97; *Captain John Smith*, 98 n. 18; *Colonial Woman's Bookshelf*, 99 n. 27

Haywood, Eliza: *Fortunate Foundlings*, 18

Heath, William Estill: "Early Colonial Money," 117 n. 108

Hemperley, Marion R., 104 n. 24

Hempstead (New York), 84

hickory, 30

Hird, Thomas, 102 n. 9

Holy Island (Great Britain), 96

Homer, 85

hominy, 46, 113 n. 83

Horace, 86; *Satires*, 89, 103 n. 20

horse, 29–30, 42, 55, 62, 107 n. 37, 117 n. 115

Horton, William, 102 n. 9

hospitality, 114 n. 85

Hughes, Merritt Y., 106 n. 35, 109 n. 49

Indians, 32, 33, 47, 61, 75, 119 nn. 128–29. *See also* individual Indian names

indentured servitude, 50–51, 117 n. 113

ipecacuana, 112 n. 70

Ivers, Larry E.: *British Drums*, 103 n. 12, 104 n. 23, 25, 107 nn. 41–42, 111 n. 63

Jackson, Harvey H.: *Forty Years of Diversity*, 110 n. 57

Jamaica, 118 n. 122

James River, 61

Jamestown (Virginia), 57

Jekyl Creek, 104 n. 24

Jekyl Island, 15, 29, 104 n. 24

Jekyl, Joseph, Sir, 104 n. 24

Jekyl Sound (St. Simons Sound), 26, 101 n. 1

Johnson, Richard, 18, 20

Johnstone, Charles, 18

Jones, Charles C., Jr., 20; *Dead Towns of Georgia*, 21, 100 n. 1

Jones, George Fenwick: *Georgia Dutch*, 103 n. 11

Jones, Hugh: *Present State of Virginia*, 117 n. 115

Jones, Noble, 21, 33, 36, 108 n. 47, 109 n. 48

juniper, 112 n. 70

Kelso, William M., 21; *Captain Jones's Wormslow*, 100 n. 44, 108 nn. 47–48; "Impermanent Architecture," 100 n. 47

Kimber, Alice, 68–69

Kimber, Edward

life: accompanies Oglethorpe's expedition to St. Augustine, 13–14; becomes editor of the *London Magazine*, 18; begins contributing poetry to the *London Magazine*, 12; birth, 11; collaborates with Richard Johnson, 18; death, 18; early life, 11; joins James Oglethorpe's regiment, 13; leaves America for Great Britain, 14–15; leaves England for America, 12–13; leaves New York, 13; reaches New York, 13; reading, 11–12; recognition of, 18–22; serves at Frederica, 14; travels from Maryland to Frederica, Georgia, 13, 43–65; visits Savannah and Charleston, 14, 35–36; voyage to Maryland, 13, 37–42; writing career, 15–18

writings: "Acrostic," 93–94; "American Song," 106 n. 32; "Annual Recess," 12; "Ballad," 89–91; *Baronetage of England*, 18; "Departure," 77–78; "Fidenia," 75–77, 118 n. 124; *General Index to ... the London Magazine*, 18, 97 n. 3, 98 n. 18; *Generous Briton*, 18; *Happy Orphans*, 17; *History of Inland Navigation*,

19; *History of the Life and Adventures of Mr. Anderson*, 17, 22, 89, 103n. 17, 106n. 32, 113n. 77, 114nn. 88 and 91, 115nn. 93–94 and 98, 117nn. 113–15, 118nn. 120; *Itinerant Observations in America*, 26–65; *Juvenile Adventures of David Ranger*, 17, 20; *Ladies Complete Letter-Writer*, 19, 66, 98n. 27, 117nn. 109 and 111; *Letter from a Citizen of London . . . Occasioned by the Late Earthquakes*, 19; "Letter from a Son," 66, 79, 80–89, 113n. 78, 118nn. 117 and 123, 121nn. 142–43; *Life and Adventures of James Ramble*, 17; *Life and Adventures of Joe Thompson*, 17, 19, 20, 116n. 108, 117n. 110, 118n. 119, 119n. 125, 120n. 134; *Life and Extraordinary Adventures of Capt. Neville Frowde*, 17; *Maria*, 18, 19, 20; "Memoirs of the Life and Writings of the Reverend Mr. Isaac Kimber," 97n. 1; "On Making Foul-Island," 94; "On the Death of Mrs. Alice Kimber," 68–69; "Parallel between the Late Earl of Peterborough and General Oglethorpe,' 15, 98n. 15; *Peerage of England*, 20; *Peerage of Ireland*, 20; *Peerage of Scotland*, 20; *Relation, or Journal of a Late Expedition*, 14, 15, 20, 21–22, 70, 97nn. 10–11, 98n. 16, 104n. 24, 119n. 128; "Repentant Deboshee," 92–93; "Song," 79–80; "Song, at New York," 13, 66–68; "To the Author of the London Magazine," 15, 98n. 15; "To the Honourable *****," 12; *Tradesman's Director*, 19; *Universal Pocket-Book*, 19; "Upon Approaching the Coast of New York," 79; "Vindication," 70–75, 92; "Written Extempore in the Castle of Edinburgh," 95; "Written on a Brick," 96

Kimber, Isaac, 11, 18, 97n. 1, 101nn. 3 and 5, 105n. 32; *Sermons*, 68, 81, 97n. 1

Kimber, Sidney A., 18, 21, 97n. 10; "Biographical Notes," 97nn. 1, 5, 6, and 8–9, 98n. 22

Kulikoff, Allan: "Origins of Afro-American Society," 100n. 47, 114n. 90

Landis, Dennis C.: *European Americana*, 98n. 19

La Rochefoucauld Liancourt, Franois Alexandre Frederic, *duc de*, 24

laurel, 30

Laurence, Kitty, 13, 66–68, 84, 88

Leith (Great Britain), 98n. 14

Lemay, J. A. Leo: *Calendar of American Poetry*, 21, 66, 68, 70, 75, 77, 79, 80, 89, 92, 93, 97n. 2, 105n. 32; *Early American Reader*, 116n. 104; "Frontiersman from Lout to Hero," 100n. 47, 118n. 119, 119n. 128; *Men of Letters in Colonial Maryland*, 97n. 2; "Southern Colonial Grotesque," 113n. 79 "Text, Tradition, and Themes of 'The Big Bear of Arkansas,'" 108n. 43

Lennox, Charlotte, 18

Lewis, Bessie Mary: "Darien, A Symbol of Defiance and Achievement," 107n. 40

Lewis, Richard: "Journey from Patapsko to Annapolis," 11, 12, 52, 105n. 32, 116n. 104, 119n. 126

Lightfoot, Philip, 62, 120n. 134

lizard, 31, 107n. 36

locust, 110n. 58

Logan, William: "Journal," 102n. 8, 116n. 101, 103

London (Great Britain), 15

London Gazette, 101n. 3

London Magazine, 11, 12, 15, 16, 23, 37, 43, 66, 68, 70, 75, 77, 79, 80, 89, 92–96, 97nn. 3–4; 98nn. 15 and 17–18, 99n. 38, 101nn. 3 and 5, 102n. 5, 105n. 32, 111nn. 66–67, 112n. 68, 113n. 78, 116n. 104

Long Island (New York), 39

Lucan, 62; *Pharsalia*, 119n. 131

Lucas, Captain, 97n. 9

Lunn, Susanna, 93–94

McDaniel, George W.: *Heart and Home*, 114n. 88

MacDonnell, Alexander R.: "The Settlement of the Scotch Highlanders at Darien," 107n. 40

Mack, Maynard, 115 n. 95
MacKall, Leonard L., 21; "Wymberley Jones De Renne Georgia Library," 99 n. 39
MacPherson, James, 107 n. 41
Magothy Bay (Magidi Bay), 57, 97 n. 8, 118 n. 120
"Malcontents," 110 n. 59
Manucy, Albert C.: *Fort at Frederica*, 100 n. 1
Martin, Peter E.: "Williamsburg," 100 n. 47
Maryland, 16, 17, 21, 22, 42–56, 75, 85, 113 n. 80, 118 nn. 115–16. *See also* references to specific creeks, forts, islands, rivers, and towns
Mein, John: *Catalogue*, 98 n. 27
Micklus, Robert: 114 n. 83
militia, 47
Milne, W. Gordon: "A Glimpse of Colonial America," 98 n. 20, 115 n. 98
Milton, John, 31, 34; *Paradise Lost*, 23, 81, 106 n. 35; *Paradise Regained*, 109 n. 49
mockingbird, 31, 105 n. 32
Monthly Review (London), 19, 99 n. 28
Morgan: "English and American Attitudes towards Convict Transportation," 115 n. 97
Morison, Samuel E., 107 n. 38
Morton, Thomas: *New English Canaan*, 108 n. 46
mosquito, 31, 103 n. 16, 107 nn. 38–39
mosses, 30
Mount Venture (Georgia), 107 n. 42
Moyle, Jeremy, 104 n. 26
mulberry, 30, 110 n. 58
mullet, 31
mush, 46
music, 56

Nantucket (Massachusetts), 83
National Union Catalog (*NUC*), 19, 98 n. 24–27
Neal, Willard: "Altamaha," 101 n. 1
Nelson, Thomas, Jr., 62, 120 n. 134
Newbould, 97 n. 6
Newcastle (Great Britain), 98 n. 4
Newfoundland, 83
New Inverness (Georgia), 32, 107 n. 40. *See also* Darien

New Jersey, 40, 112 n. 71
New York (New York), 17, 38, 66–68
Nightingale (ship), 97 n. 6
Norbury, Richard, 103 n. 13
Norfolk (Virginia), 57, 63, 120 n. 137
Northampton County (Virginia), 56
Northhampton (Virginia), 97 n. 8
Nurten (Nutten, Nutting, or Governors Island), 38, 112 n. 70

oak, 30, 105 n. 28
Ocmulgee River, 101 n. 1
Oconee River, 101 n. 1
O'Connell, Neil J.: "George Whitefield and Bethesda Orphan-House," 109 n. 55
Ogeechee River, 104 n. 27, 107 n. 41
Oglethorpe, James, 15, 27, 36, 70, 85, 89, 102 nn. 8 and 9, 103 n. 14, 115 n. 92; brings Indians to England, 119 n. 129; builds road between Fort Frederica and Fort St. Simons, 102 n. 7; establishes Fort Frederica, 100 n. 1; expedition to St. Augustine, Florida, 13; has lighthouse built at Tybee, 111 n. 62; home on St. Simons Island ("The Farm,"), 102 n. 10; orders Captain MacPherson to build Fort Argyle, 107 n. 41; policy against importing slaves or rum, 110 n. 59; relations with German emigrants, 102 n. 1; returns from England, 104 n. 23; settles St. Simons Island, 104 n. 23; treaty with Creek Indians, 108 n. 44; verse tributes to, 79–80
olive, 30, 110 n. 58
opossum, 31, 105 n. 30
orange, 102 n. 8, 103 n. 16, 110 n. 58
Orkneys (Great Britain), 15, 98 n. 14
Ossebaw Island (Georgia), 104 n. 41, 108 n. 44
Oxford English Dictionary, 101 n. 2
oyster, 31

palmetto, 28, 103 n. 17
parakeet, 60
Pares, Richard: *War and Trade in the Wets Indies*, 104 n. 22, 114 n. 87
partridge, 32
peach, 30, 102 n. 8, 103 n. 16, 110 n. 58

Pennsylvania, 37, 57
"Peregrinus Vespusianus" (pseud.).
  See Kimber, Edward
persimmon, 44, 45, 113 n. 79
Pike, Richard, 103 n. 14
Pike's Bluff, 28, 103 n. 14
Pindar, 12
pine, 30
plum, 110 n. 58
Pocomoke River, 113 n. 80
Poe, Edgar Allan: *Narrative of Arthur
  Gordon Pym,* 13
pomegranate, 30, 102 n. 8
Pope, Alexander, 49; *Essay on Man,*
  115 n. 95; "Windsor Forest," 12
porpoise, 31, 58, 61
Portobello (Panama), 104 n. 22
Port Royal, 111 n. 64
Port Royal Island (South Carolina),
  36, 98 n. 13
Port Royal River, 111 n. 63
Port Royal Sound, 36
Potosi (Bolivia), 49, 115 n. 96
prickly-pear shrub, 30
Prince, Thomas, 109 n. 50
Prior, Matthew, 12
purslane, 103 n. 21

Rabelais, François, 54, 117 n. 110
rabbit, 32–33
raccoon, 31, 105 n. 31
red-bird, 31
Reese, Trevor: *Frederica,* 100 n. 1;
  Clamorous Malconents, 110 n. 59
religion, 53
Reps, John W.: "C² + L² = S²?," 110 n.
  57; *Tidwater Towns,* 120 n. 137
rice, 13 n. 82
Riley, Edward M.: "Colonial Courthouses," 99 n. 38, 120 n. 135; "Suburban Development of Yorktown,"
  120 n. 134, 121 n. 138
Roscoe, S. John: *John Newberry,*
  99 n. 31
Rowe, Nicholas, 119 n. 119

St. Augustine (Florida), 13–14, 22,
  104 n. 22
St. Catherine's Island (Georgia), 33,
  104 n. 27, 108 nn. 44 and 48
St. Simons Island, 13, 15, 26–29, 65,

97 n. 9, 102 nn. 9 and 11, 103 n. 14,
  104 nn. 23–25
Salzburgers, 27, 102 n. 11
sand-bird, 106 n. 33
sand-fly, 31
Sandy Hook (New Jersey), 38, 79, 84,
  112 n. 71
Sapelo Island, 104 n. 27, 108 n. 44
Sarah's Creek, 57
sassafras, 30
Savannah (Georgia), 14, 32, 33, 35–
  36, 98 n. 13, 109 n. 56, 110 nn. 57–58
  and 60, 111 nn. 61–62
Saye, Albert B.: *List of the Early Settlers,* 104 n. 25
Scottish Highlanders, 107 n. 40
Scroggs, Robert, 103 n. 12
servitude, indentured, 50–51, 117 n.
  113
Shakespeare, William, 12
sheep, 42
Sheridan, Frances, 18
Shetland, 98 n. 14
"Short Account of the British Planta-
  tions in America," 98 n. 18
Sinepuxent (Maryland), 17, 37, 42,
  44, 89, 113 n. 77, 118 n. 120
Sirmans, M. Eugene: *Colonial South
  Carolina,* 115 n. 92, 116 n. 107
Skaggs, David Curtis, 113 n. 81
skunk, 14
slaves and slavery, 38–40, 43, 48–49,
  75–77, 114 n. 88–89, 115 nn. 92–93,
  117 n. 114
Smith, Abbot Emerson: *Colonists in
  Bondage,* 115 n. 97
Smith, Henry A. M.: "Beaufort,"
  111 n. 65
Snow Hill (Maryland), 13, 44, 51, 57,
  113 n. 80, 116 n. 101 and 103
Somerset County (Maryland), 113 n.
  80
South Carolina, 16, 17, 37, 47, 101 n.
  2, 104 n. 25, 115 n. 92, 116 n. 107.
  See also references to specific
  creeks, forts, islands, rivers, and
  towns
Spain, 22, 27, 101 n. 1, 104 nn. 23
  and 25
Spalding, Phinzy: *Forty Years of Di-*

versity, 110n. 57; *Oglethorpe in America*, 119n. 129
Spectator, 12, 77
spinach, 108n. 45
Spotswood, Alexander, 114n. 87
squirrel, 31, 105n. 31
Stedman, Captain?, 98n. 14
Stephens, William, 36, 110n. 60; *Journal*, 109n. 53, 110nn. 56 and 60, 111n. 64
Stevens, William (colonel), 113n. 80
Stevens, William Bacon: "Sketch of the Life of James Habersham," 109n. 54
stingray, 31
Stiverson, Gregory A.: "Virginia in 1732," 99n. 42, 120nn. 133 and 135–36
Stone, Garry Wheeler: "Impermanent Architecture," 100n. 47
Sutherland, Patrick: *Account of the Late Invasion of Georgia*, 101n. 3
Swem, Earl: "Views of Yorktown and Gloucester," 21, 99n. 40, 119n. 132
Swift, Jonathan, 12

tabby (tappy), 26, 101n. 2
Tacitus, 119n. 128
Tatler, 77
Temple, Sarah B. Gober: *Georgia Journeys*, 108n. 47, 110n. 58, 111nn. 61–62
Tepaske, John Jay, 97n. 11
tobacco, 46, 57–58, 113n. 75
Tocqueville, Alexis de, 24
Tomochichi, 119n. 129
Toonahowi, 61, 119n. 129
Trollope, Anthony, 24
True and Historical Narrative of the Colony of Georgia, 110n. 59
Trustees' Garden (Savannah), 36, 110n. 58
turkey, 32, 60, 107n. 43
turtledove, 31, 60
Two Sisters (ship), 98n. 14
Tybee Island, 36, 111n. 62
Tyler, Lyon Gardiner: *Encyclopedia of Virginia Biography*, 117n. 112, 120n. 134, 121n. 141

Upton, Dell: "Impermanent Architecture," 100n. 47; "White and Black Landscapes," 100n. 47, 114n. 88
Utley, Francis Lee, 104n. 24

Vaughan, Alden T., 108n. 46
Verelst, Cornelis, 119n. 129
Vernon, Edward, 104n. 22, 114n. 87
Vernon River, 110n. 60
Virgil, 85; *Aeneid*, 29, 103n. 20
Virginia, 16, 17, 22, 46, 47, 52, 54, 56–65, 85, 118n. 115, 118. *See also* references to specific creeks, forts, islands, rivers, and towns
Virginia Gazette Daybooks, 98n. 27

Waldman, Carl: *Who Was Who in Native American History*, 119n. 129
Walker, Keith, 114n. 86
Waller, Edmund, 12
walnut, 30
Watt, Robert: *Bibliotheca Britannica*, 20, 99n. 33
Weekly Register (London), 11, 116n. 104
West Indies, 46, 63, 112n. 69
Weston, Willes, 102n. 9
Whiffen, Marcus: *Eighteenth-Century Houses of Williamsburg*, 121n. 140; *Public Building of Williamsburg*, 121n. 140
Whitby, Captain?, 98n. 14
Whitefield, George, 33, 109n. 53. *See also* Bethesda Orphan House
Whitelaw, Ralph T., 118n. 118
William and Mary, College of, 54–55, 63, 117n. 112
Williamsburg (Virginia), 13, 54, 63–64, 121n. 140
Williams, W. R.: "British-American Officers," 102n. 8, 103n. 13
Winsor, Justin: *Narrative and Critical History*, 99n. 37
Wise, Jennings Cropper: *Ye Kingdome of Accawmacke*, 118n. 118
wolf, 31
woodcock, 106n. 33
woodtick, 32
Wood, William: *New England's Prospect*, 108n. 46
Worcester County (Maryland), 45, 113n. 80, 118n. 115

Wormsloe, 21, 33, 97n. 13, 108nn. 47–48
Wotton, Thomas: *Baronetage of England*, 18
Wright, Louis B., 105n. 32

Yamasee Indians, 107n. 42, 119n. 129

Yentsch, Anne Elizabeth: *Chesapeake Family*, 100n. 47
York River, 57, 61
Yorktown (Virginia), 13, 21, 57, 62–63, 97n. 8, 119n. 132, 120nn. 133–35, 121n. 138